LEADERSHIP IN ACTION II

INFLUENTIAL IRISH MEN NURSES' CONTRIBUTION TO SOCIETY

Edited by
Geraldine McCarthy & Joyce J. Fitzpatrick

Published by OAK TREE PRESS, 19 Rutland Street, Cork, Ireland
www.oaktreepress.com

A catalogue record of this book is available from the British Library.

ISBN 978 1 78119 101 9 (Paperback)
ISBN 978 1 78119 102 6 (ePub)
ISBN 978 1 78119 103 3 (Kindle)

Cover design: Kieran O'Connor
Cover image: Igor Goncharenko / 123rf.com

Printed in Ireland by SPRINT-print Ltd.

CONTENTS

PREFACE

This book is a companion to the book we published in 2012: *Leadership in Action: Influential Irish Women Nurses' Contribution to Society*. Even at the time of our first discussion of profiling the women nurse leaders who had made significant contributions, we had a hunch that it would not be long before we followed with this volume of men in Irish nursing who had made lasting contributions through their lives and work. We just were not sure it would be so soon!

The 19 leaders profiled in this book have made significant contributions to nursing, health care and society. Several of them have extended their work beyond national boundaries to the international arena. All of them began their careers as nurses. As will be noted, many of the men started as psychiatric mental health nurses, as this entry was often viewed as more favourable to men who wanted to enter the nursing profession. Some, but not all, of the men describe the gender discrimination they experience in a profession dominated by women. This is a gender theme that persists in the nursing literature today.

The book is a tribute to the nurses whose lives are profiled in each chapter. Their contributions are noteworthy and their advice for promising leaders throughout nursing and health care should be heeded. As with the previous book on women nurse leaders, we have selected an apposite quote from each person interviewed and highlighted it at the beginning of the chapter. A collection of these quotes alone would provide instruction on leadership.

We thank each of the leaders who were interviewed for this book. Each of them gave generously of their time, just as they each have dedicated their talents and skills to making a difference in the world in which they live and work. Their dedication to others is particularly impressive.

We also wish to acknowledge and thank the nurses who conducted the interviews. For some of the doctoral students who participated in the project, this represents their first professional publication. They are all aspiring leaders. Others who have participated are members of the staff of the Catherine McCauley School of Nursing & Midwifery, University College Cork. They are leading the way, influencing students and colleagues daily in the pursuit of knowledge. Together, we are all students of leadership, each learning each day, from each other.

We wish to acknowledge especially the work of Elizabeth Weathers, as Research Assistant, in the typing and drafting of this book.

And last, but not least, we acknowledge the financial support of An Bord Altranais, which made publication of this book possible.

The nursing profession is rich in history, and as the testimonies in this book support, each nurse has touched thousands of lives. We continue to marvel at the ripple effect of the leadership accomplishments of those who began their careers in nursing.

Geraldine McCarthy and Joyce J. Fitzpatrick
April 2013

CHAPTER 1

INTRODUCTION:
PERSPECTIVES ON LEADERSHIP

Geraldine McCarthy and Joyce J. Fitzpatrick

Leadership is a familiar topic in management and professional courses. Theoretical and practical perspectives on leadership abound. From a review of Internet sites, one can easily find a wide range of continuing education and self-help programmes designed to help individuals beginning and advanced leadership skills.

Leadership courses frequently are embedded in academic and professional degree programmes. As academics, we have taught leadership to hundreds of students. A kaleidoscopic view of theories of leadership that are predominant in health sciences programmes includes transactional and transformational models, principled-centred leadership, servant leadership, quantum leadership, situational leadership, and leadership practices.

One of the most important components in understanding leadership is assessing one's own values. Leaders and those who aspire to leadership should engage in self-assessment, not only to clarify their values but also to know what skills they currently possess and those that will require development and/or refinement. Through self-assessment exercises, leaders also can identify their competencies and determine the best fit in relation to prospective positions.

Career planning is also important for aspiring leaders. Building on the self-assessment, aspiring leaders can select mentors to help them to round out their skills and abilities. While not all leaders identify key mentors in their career development, most do identify influential persons who helped to guide their careers. The American College of Healthcare Executives (ACHE) identifies several resources for developing mentoring relationships, both for the leader who is serving as mentor as well as for the protégé (ACHE, 2011). These include basic guides about the value and benefits of mentoring, the basics of mentoring relationships, and the creation of a career learning plan to extend beyond the mentoring relationship.

One of the most comprehensive perspectives on leadership that has dominated the leadership literature in the last decade is the work of Kouzes & Posner (2008). Over a period of 20 years, Kouzes & Posner gathered the views of 75,000 people to determine the common characteristics of leaders. The top five characteristics identified included honesty; forward-looking; competent; inspiring; and intelligent. Kouzes & Posner then developed the five actions that they considered key to successful leadership: model the way; inspire a shared vision; challenge the process; enable others to act; and encourage the heart. Further, they developed the Leadership Practices Inventory (LPI), which can be used to assess these leadership characteristics. The LPI has been used in research across a range of disciplines; it also can be used as a self-assessment tool for aspiring leaders.

Another important leadership perspective is that of quantum leadership, developed by Porter-O'Grady & Malloch (2010). They identify key skills for leaders in nursing and health care including: complexity, emotional competence, conflict management and transformational skills. Further, these authors present a view that innovation should be a way of life for leaders. They also present key principles for the quantum leader (Malloch & Porter-O'Grady, 2009). These include: viewing the organisation as a complex mosaic; creating the broadest possible vision; managing information and dynamics; understanding the uncertainty and paradox of transformation; understanding both the formal and informal networks; and understanding the most important part of systems as their intersections (Malloch & Porter-O'Grady, pp. 1-19).

In learning to lead, individuals must build networks and coalitions. They must understand the flow of the organisations in which they work, and the need for interfaces with the many others who also are part of the organisation, including those within the formal and informal networks.

In summary, a number of models exist that describe and predict leadership characteristics and behaviours. In the following chapters, the contributors developed profiles of Irish men who have contributed to society and health care, having begun their careers as nurses. Each of the profiles includes the early influences and major life events that shaped the leader; the person's vision for their life work; their competencies, strengths and values; the significant challenges that they experienced; opportunities that enhanced their success; their perspective on the characteristics of leaders; and their advice to aspiring leaders. Importantly, these profiles provide a snapshot in time of the significant contributions of these leaders.

REFERENCES

American College of Healthcare Executives (2011). *Career Resource Center: Leadership in Mentoring.* Accessed 8 December 2011 from http://www.ache.org/newclub/career/MentorArticles/Mentoring.cfm.

Kouzes, J.M. & Posner, B.Z. (2008). *The Leadership Challenge* (4th ed.), San Francisco, CA: Jossey-Bass.

Malloch, K. & Porter-O'Grady, T. (2009). *The Quantum Leader: Applications for the New World of Work* (2nd ed.), Massachusetts: Jones & Bartlett.

Porter-O'Grady, T. & Malloch, K. (2010). *Quantum Leadership* (3rd ed.), Massachusetts: Jones & Bartlett.

CHAPTER 2
IAN CARTER

Sean Kelleher

If you can't measure it, you can't manage it.

Ian Carter was born in Monmouth, Wales and spent his school years in Hereford. He is the Chief Executive Officer (CEO) at St. James's Hospital, a 998-bed academic teaching hospital in Dublin. Ian has held senior hospital management positions in Ireland (St. James's Hospital and Mid-Western Health Board); in England (Director of Contracts & Business Administration, 1st Wave Hospital Trust); and in Saudi Arabia (Assistant Hospital Manager).

He holds corporate responsibility for St. James's Quality Programme and has developed significant accreditation, patient advocacy, risk management and performance indicator programmes, including the establishment of an international academic teaching hospital performance benchmarking initiative, which he currently chairs. He also has led the design and execution of a series of interlinked initiatives within primary and secondary care designed to improve hospital capability/capacity in terms of patient processing. For the last seven years, Ian also has held the post of Associate Lecturer, National College of Ireland, with specific interest in organisational behaviour management theory. He has recently begun a PhD in secondary care performance metrics.

EARLY INFLUENCES

Ian's mother was the biggest influence on his life. She worked in local politics and was vice chairman of a local health authority in the United Kingdom (UK), which imbued within her a strong sense of altruism. Ian feels that he may have developed a public sector ethos and enjoyment in understanding the rewards of working with people from his mother.

Ian's father was a metallurgist and physicist and never really understood Ian's interest in wanting to work within the health sector, in particular his decision to become a nurse. Ian attributes this to his father being a 'lab animal', who did not really appreciate life outside of the laboratory. His father left the family when Ian was 14, thus he was not available to offer any constructive career guidance.

On leaving school, Ian originally wanted to pursue a career in medicine, but he was convinced to consider nursing as a more favourable option by friends who had already trained as nurses and extolled its many benefits, not least the opportunity to travel and study in London. As an 18-year old country boy, the big city lights proved very enticing. Ian undertook a three-year registered general nursing programme in St. Joseph's Hospital, in Tooting Broadway. Six months post-qualification, he transferred to the old Atkinson Morley Hospital in Wimbledon, noted at that time as one of the most advanced brain surgery centres in the world, to begin a course in neurosciences. On completion of the programme, he was promoted to Charge Nurse and subsequently to the position of Senior Clinical Nurse Specialist for Neurosciences. This upward trajectory continued with his appointment to the post of Manager of Cardio-thoracic and Neurosciences Surgery.

On reflection, Ian recalls that this was a time of rapid adjustment, particularly the transition from a 'hands on' clinical specialist to that of a clinical manager. While he thoroughly enjoyed the clinical contact with patients, it was ultimately the dynamics of management that fascinated him. Ian's ability to manage teams of people to realise specific goals and outcomes was a trait he seemed to hold even as a student nurse, one that evidently did not go unnoticed as he continued to assume general management positions in the UK, Saudi Arabia and Ireland. Ian secured his current position as CEO of St. James's Hospital in 2007. Prior to this appointment, he was deputy CEO of St. James's and general manager of the Mid-Western General Hospital in Limerick.

School had a considerable impact on Ian's decision to pursue a career in health care. There were also a number of people and life events that influenced Ian's adult life: Margaret, his partner of 20 years, who is a Midwifery lecturer in Trinity College Dublin, had a major impact on the trajectory of his career; his close friends and respected peers were also an influence. Ian recalls a figure from the early 1980s, a nurse manager who successfully managed the bridge from being the conventional old-fashioned matron type to a dynamic inpatient services manager. This was at a time in the UK when there was recognition that the health system needed generic management skills and that some of those generic skills could best be found within nursing because nurses generally seemed to have a slightly broader perspective on patient care.

Others who have had a positive influence on Ian include Eilísh Hardiman,[1] John O'Brien, and Mary Harney. As Director of Nursing in St. James's, Eilísh had a very strong influence on the system and in the development of the role of the nurse. Eilísh helped to create the structures to allow the development of

---

[1]   **Chapter 10**, *Leadership in Action: Influential Irish Women Nurses' Contribution to Society*, Geraldine McCarthy & Joyce J. Fitzpatrick, Oak Tree Press, 2012.

'ambidextrous nurses': nurses who could work anywhere, with a very strong likelihood that wherever placed they would thrive and develop a high capacity to adapt to various situations. John O'Brien, Ian's previous boss, was a clear thinker and had the ability to crystallise problems and find solutions. Mary Harney, former Minister for Health, was in Ian's opinion a clear thinker and had a remarkable ability to express her ideas and thoughts with accuracy, an ability that Ian admired regardless of whether he always agreed with her ideas.

Ian also has a great admiration of advanced nurse practitioners and the energy they bring to nursing and patient care. He believes that the best person to manage your care should be somebody who spends his or her entire time performing that particular facet of care and whether he or she is a physician or a nurse should not matter.

MAJOR LIFE EVENTS

Ian acknowledges his experience of working in Saudi Arabia as being very formative. He suggests that, if you ever want to develop generic management skills, you should move to a different culture with a different language and have a war break out at the same time (the invasion of Kuwait) and try to apply your management abilities in a radically different environment. In his case, it was 1990 and he was recruited as Assistant Hospital Manager in a private hospital in Riyadh specifically to introduce a Western management ethos to the hospital. After six months, Iraq invaded Kuwait, with significant repercussions for Saudi Arabia. In the turmoil, Ian was asked to temporarily run one of the Sheik's engineering companies located next door to the hospital, which he recalls as being an invaluable learning experience.

CONTRIBUTION TO NURSING

Ian is hesitant to identify his specific contribution to nursing. He recalls that, when he was a clinical nurse specialist, he was a very strong proponent of education, was involved in teaching in various hospitals and an advocate for ensuring that nursing staff were exposed to educational opportunities. At that time, the average nurse did not receive a graduate education, and most nurses underwent a three-year apprenticeship that arguably provided less theory than was required. In his various management roles, Ian's contributions relate more to ensuring that specific outcomes were achieved. More recently, he has become a strong believer in the concept 'if you can't measure it, then you can't manage it', as espoused by William Edwards Deming. According to Ian, in Ireland we tend to describe what we do as nurses or managers and do not necessarily focus as much on the outcomes. Ian wants to change this and is trying, in so far as possible, to introduce an outcomes culture ethos within St. James's.

Ian believes that, while he may have contributed in some degree to nursing, nursing itself has contributed significantly to the person he is and the things he has achieved. He believes that nursing provides people with a very broad educational platform, which makes one eminently suitable for a career in health management, mainly because it provides a very good understanding of the patient.

VISION FOR YOUR LIFE'S WORK

Vision is something Ian has not really considered in much depth. He enjoys his current management position. St. James's Hospital is at the cutting edge of health care provision and managing it is very demanding. At the same time, his position offers a unique opportunity to affect the progression of a large and influential organisation, which is rewarding. He works with the brightest and the best from so many professional fields and believes that, together, they are creating a system that is responsive to patients' needs. Ian would be very content to complete his working life in St. James's Hospital.

COMPETENCIES, STRENGTHS AND VALUES

Ian considers his main strengths to be resilience, a good sense of humour, a career-guided purpose, a sense of vision, and the ability to see a new picture and translate it into something that is meaningful for whichever member of staff or group he is dealing with. He tries to always look ahead and consider the future in most of his decision-making.

As a manager, Ian says it is important to recognise that successful systems work best when you are looking forward as opposed to sideways or backwards, and then figuring out how to get the team to move forward voluntarily. This can happen only if you have a passion for what you are doing. Most of us, Ian contends, like to be in equilibrium, and while it is said that change is good, in Ian's experience most people do not welcome change – they like stability and harmony. Ian believes that people need to learn to recognise the potential in change and endorse and welcome it, particularly in an unstable environment.

CHARACTERISTICS OF LEADERS

A leader must have a passion to affect change, combined with a sense of vision, an ability to analyse situations and well-developed communication skills. Ian believes that it is erroneous to consider leadership skills and management abilities as being separate qualities and says that, to be a senior executive, you have to have both management and leadership experience and ability. While management training gives you theoretical models or programmes that can be aligned to or blended within a system, leaders have an ability to synthesise and conceptualise at a high level and to translate their ideas into something tangible and desirable for others.

SIGNIFICANT CHALLENGES

Currently, Ireland is facing very serious challenges in public expenditure. Ian maintains that this may be advantageous, as when you introduce extreme fiscal instability in any system there is a strong likelihood that decisions become clearer because of the limited number of choices. For example, it is now very evident that the health sector in Ireland was not as structured and focused as believed. Consider the Health Service Executive, for example: once considered a great bastion of success, it is now being dismantled because it did not work despite the exorbitant amount of money and energy invested.

The current economic crisis means that health service managers, such as Ian, must manage with less. Unpalatable decisions have to be made, which may result in deterioration in performance despite what politicians say. There are approximately 50 hospitals in the country with a very large amount of labour and money tied up in simply running these 50 organisations. Rationalisation and descaling is inevitable, which if done correctly may be of benefit but otherwise could leave untold chaos in its wake.

OPPORTUNITIES THAT ENHANCED SUCCESS

Ian believes that being a nurse has helped his success because, as a nurse, you develop a very good understanding of patient care, of multidisciplinary teams and of how hospitals work. While these abilities can be learned, it is not the same as actually having experienced them.

There is, however, also a flip side. You can end up with professional baggage that needs to be channelled, but generally these experiences are very important in helping you to make balanced and important decisions.

OBSTACLES ENCOUNTERED AND LESSONS LEARNED

The impetuosity of youth is an obstacle that springs to mind and the compulsion to do things without giving them much consideration. Ian feels that, with maturity, one adopts a more logical and structured approach. He believes that the biggest obstacle to any form of change is probably not understanding the problem in the first place and coming up with a solution that does not work. The solution is wrong because you have not identified the actual problem. This is likely a problem for most managers, if they are honest.

ADVICE TO ASPIRING LEADERS

Ian is tentative in offering advice to anybody who would like to pursue a career in management in the health sector; rather he would prefer to offer a commentary. Health care is probably one of the most complex areas of employment. It has many and multiple layers of stakeholders and it does not necessarily work with a sense of logic in terms of how things are done, despite the public's perceptions. Many of the processes used are tried and tested. We talk about individualised patient care; however, most patients will have the same care as the previous person with the same condition. It is helpful to consider health care management as a dance: a dance with established patterns and steps. If the steps are followed, then more often than not, you will look as though you are dancing; however, it is the passion for the dance, and a person's sense of rhythm, that distinguishes the good from the bad.

If you want to be successful in health care management, you need to listen to what the patient is saying – the irony, however, is that the further up the 'ivory tower' you go, the easier it is to become removed from patients, but this would be to your peril. A few years ago, Ian set up a group to advise him on what it is actually like being a patient in St. James's. Ian values the feedback received as he believes that it is very important to have personalised accounts from those who are affected by health care. Health care management in a large public sector is a bureaucracy and if you want to affect change, ultimately you need to have a degree of patience with the bureaucracy.

CHAPTER 3
PATRICK COTTER

Malitha Veera Monis

Be patient, but persistent.
Anything worthwhile is worth the effort.

Patrick Cotter was born in Cork and is the eldest of seven children. He has five brothers and one sister. He is married to Riona and has two children: a daughter, Hannah, and a son, David.

Patrick completed his Diploma in General Nursing in the Cork Voluntary Hospitals School of Nursing, Cork. He was the first male student based at South Infirmary Victoria University Hospital,

Cork (SIVUH). Patrick also trained as a midwife at the Cork College of Midwifery. On completion, he returned to a permanent post at SIVUH, working in the emergency department. Patrick holds a Diploma in Management and Employee Relations (National College of Ireland); a Postgraduate Diploma in Emergency Nursing (University College Cork (UCC), 2001); a BSc Nursing Studies (UCC, 2003) and a MSc Nursing Studies (UCC, 2005). Patrick spent two years lecturing in University College Cork (2003 to 2005) and then registered as an Advanced Nurse Practitioner (ANP) in the Emergency Department in Cork University Hospital where he now works. He also holds a position as Adjunct Lecturer in the Catherine McCauley School of Nursing & Midwifery in UCC. Patrick has a Certificate in Clinical Diagnostic Skills for Advanced Nurse Practitioners in Emergency Nursing (St. James's Hospital, Dublin); a Certificate for Nurse Prescribing of Medical Products (University College Cork); and a Certificate in Nurse Prescribing of Ionizing Radiation (Health Service Executive). He is presently undertaking a Doctorate in Nursing at UCC.

EARLY INFLUENCES

Patrick says his first and foremost influence was his mother. Being the eldest of seven children meant that he assisted in the care of his younger siblings. His mother is credited with showing him how to be resourceful and caring and the value of effort and hard work. Schoolteachers also influenced him, especially a secondary school science teacher who instilled a love of science in every student.

Patrick's experience working with the St. John's Ambulance Brigade was another influence. He remembers one particular officer who nurtured and developed his potential, resulting in improvements in his confidence. This officer even suggested that Patrick undertake a diploma in nursing.

He refers to the management style, caring attitude and organising skills of his first Director of Nursing as having a great influence on him, as the Director placed faith in Patrick sometimes assigning him the responsibility of Charge Nurse or acting Assistant Director. Patrick also recalls past ward sisters and managers who helped him and encouraged him along the way. In addition, he cites one particular Professor of Nursing who has influenced him and continues to influence him today.

Patrick says that one valuable lesson he has learned from these nurse leaders is not to contemplate the negative experiences in life. All of the above influences have inspired him with the qualities needed to take up life challenges. Patrick reveals that people have shown great faith in him, encouraged him to take responsibility, instilled confidence and worked as significant confidence-builders.

MAJOR LIFE EVENTS

Patrick says he did not intend to enter the nursing profession until his final year in secondary school when he was undertaking the Leaving Certificate. At that time, there were not many men in nursing, and he was studying in an all-boys school. During a career guidance programme, a teacher gave him a booklet on nursing careers that explained how to join nursing in the United Kingdom. As part of hospital duty with the St. John's Ambulance Brigade, Patrick helped in the Emergency Department and also assisted on the general wards with patient mobilisation and transport. One particular nurse took an interest in encouraging him to apply for nursing. Patrick regards his acceptance into nursing and his time training as a midwife as major life events. The skills he learned as part of his midwifery training still help him with patient care today.

CONTRIBUTION TO NURSING

Patrick says that his clinical experience caring for patients over the past 21 years is his contribution to nursing. Additionally, he has been involved in education of students, both in the academic and clinical settings. He was the site co-ordinator for the introduction of Nurse Prescribing of Medicinal Products in Cork University Hospital. He also was involved in introducing and developing Advanced Nursing Practice in the Cork/ Kerry region.

VISION FOR YOUR LIFE'S WORK

According to Patrick, the broad vision for his life work is to influence nursing care and the nursing profession, and to strive for enhanced patient care. Realising true potential is very important in achieving his goal and he expresses concern that there appears to be a gap between nursing education, nursing research and clinical practice. He acknowledges that, within the nursing profession, we have superb scholars and expert researchers, but the most effective team will be the one that includes both clinicians and researchers. Further integration of clinical practice and research will enhance the development of clinical nursing knowledge and the patient and the nursing profession will reap the benefits.

COMPETENCIES, STRENGTHS, AND VALUES

Patrick considers himself a hard-working, dedicated and committed individual. He has the ability to think of the bigger picture. He can contribute his nursing knowledge to patient care. He is clinically competent at an expert level, as he has to manage the care of a patient from the moment that patient enters hospital, until their discharge or referral. He is also competent in clinical teaching and in academia. He values honesty and commitment, as well as hard work. He also values caring for his patients, students and colleagues. He considers his dedication and commitment to the profession as his strengths. His focus is always on excellence in patient care.

CHARACTERISTICS OF LEADERS

Patrick says that a good leader is always visible to colleagues; cares about the people around them; has experience with patients; is willing to make unpopular, but correct, decisions; and has the ability to work hard and lead by example. A leader is a person who has a vision for the profession but is also politically astute in order to achieve their vision. There are some leaders who influenced him negatively – for example, invisible leaders, who lacked communication skills and often followed a populist approach. These leaders fail to make decisions, especially when the decision may be unpopular.

SIGNIFICANT CHALLENGES

Patrick says he has faced some difficulties during his professional life, but he considers all of them as challenges. The first and foremost challenge was to gain entry into nursing. Another challenge was that of being a male in a female-dominated profession.

In recent years, Patrick had to liaise and negotiate with interdisciplinary professionals in order to negotiate his role as an ANP. He had to contest boundaries of other health care disciplines. Patrick undertook this task in a cautious manner to avoid disrupting patient care by maintaining interpersonal relationships and not breaking referral pathways. It took some time for Patrick's role as ANP to be integrated into the multidisciplinary team, as it was sometimes regarded as a threat to the role of other health care providers. However, it is apparent now that his role as ANP is beneficial to patient care because, depending on the complaint, the patient is usually reviewed much quicker and receives comprehensive care from a single professional.

Patrick also refers to the major challenge of trying to balance all aspects of life – for example, clinical work, teaching, education, and family. He suggests that the ability to sustain commitments in the work-life balance is the most important, but also the most challenging, aspect. Patrick pays tribute to his wife for her endless support in all his efforts.

OPPORTUNITIES THAT ENHANCED SUCCESS

Patrick states that he has tried to avail of all opportunities that have come his way. The first opportunity was when he successfully applied for nursing. Another example is as a result of being involved in a university project, which led him to apply for and obtain a lecturing post. Patrick attributes the many employment opportunities that he received to his own educational efforts, such as obtaining a Master's degree and studying for a Doctorate in Nursing. He availed of opportunities when they presented themselves and his sound educational background made him ready to accept responsibilities, develop new programmes, engage in research and contribute to the profession in every possible way. He is grateful to the Commission on Nursing, which afforded nurses the potential to develop their clinical career pathways. He also says he is thankful to all the leaders who paved the way for his success.

OBSTACLES ENCOUNTERED AND LESSONS LEARNED

Patrick has never considered anything as an obstacle; instead, he refers to 'challenges encountered'. He says that such challenges must be directly confronted to negotiate a mutually agreed way forward. His concern is that, in the nursing profession, clinical practice, education and research should go hand-in-hand. He acknowledges that the integration and intertwining of knowledge between nurse researchers and nurse practitioners will lead to the provision of evidence-based care and a holistic approach to patient care.

ADVICE TO ASPIRING LEADERS

Patrick's advice to aspiring leaders is to keep the patient always as a centre of your focus, whether you are in clinical practice, education or research.

CHAPTER 4
SEAMUS COWMAN

Catrina Heffernan

The roots of education are bitter but the fruits are sweet.

Seamus Cowman, Professor of Nursing and Head of Department, Faculty of Nursing & Midwifery, Royal College of Surgeons in Ireland (RCSI), was born and reared in Kiltealy, a village in north Wexford. He is the eldest of a family of six and has five sisters. Seamus began his psychiatric nurse training at St. Patrick's Hospital, Dublin in 1976 and did his general nurse training at Epsom Hospital, Surrey. Subsequently, he worked as a Staff Nurse in an Intensive Care Unit (ICU) and undertook a two-year Diploma in Nursing offered by the Royal College of Nursing, University of London. He became interested in student education, which led to his appointment as a clinical teacher and as an acting Nurse Tutor. He completed a Postgraduate Certificate in Education for Adults (PGCEA) at the University of Surrey and a MSc in Education. He returned to Dublin in 1985 and completed his PhD at Dublin City University.

EARLY INFLUENCES

Seamus attended a secondary school in Bunclody, Co. Wexford. It was a girls' boarding school and Seamus was among the first cohort of Leaving Certificate boys in the school. It was run by nuns and he believes that the regime taught him a great deal. Values were very different at that time – for example discipline, tolerance and respect – which greatly contributed to his interpersonal development and helped form him in his career. As regards the influences on his career choice, his first cousin, Mary Hughes, then a nurse in St. James's Hospital, was influential in encouraging him to choose nursing. She was just qualifying as a nurse when he was doing his Leaving Certificate. Mary's father, John O'Neill, was a psychiatric nurse at St. Senan's Hospital in Enniscorthy, Co. Wexford. He also was influential in reassuring Seamus that psychiatric nursing was a good career choice.

Seamus staffed for one year in psychiatric nursing before embarking on a career in general nursing in England. Ms Annie Kelly, the Matron of St. Patrick's Hospital, guided him greatly by highlighting standards and professionalism. She was very fair and dealt with people in a very gentle and humane way. She knew everything that was happening to staff and patients and was a positive role model.

Experiences at St. Patrick's Hospital, Dublin influenced his nursing career. Here he learnt the basic skills of life, dealing with all human activity, providing psychiatric services, and how to become confident, autonomous, and creative. He enjoyed the work at St. Patrick's and was very involved in sporting activities in Dublin. He was comfortable in this position and could have easily stayed in Dublin, like so many of his friends.

However, he made a decision in the summer of 1977 to travel to London and work as a nurse there. A different culture offered new experiences. He met individuals with a totally different attitude, which contributed greatly to his professional development, his nursing career, and to making him who he is today. Seamus encourages newly qualifying nurses to travel and obtain experience of other cultures, health services and nursing.

In the 1970s, there was little focus on discrimination and it was quite acceptable to refuse students on the basis of gender and so Seamus was refused entry to a number of programmes. He retains the letters from hospitals in Ireland refusing him a place in general nursing as a reminder of that bygone era. Seamus was accompanied to England by three other male colleagues, who had similar experiences in attempting to obtain a general nurse training education. They went to Epsom Hospital in Surrey and completed their general nurse training in an apprenticeship-style programme. He acquired great confidence in clinical nursing and was invited by the School of Nursing to give some lectures. He was asked to introduce the 'nursing process' into a long-stay care of the elderly hospital in Surrey. Both the staff and patients were institutionalised. It was a tough assignment as no one had heard about the nursing process. It was there that he gained an appreciation of what Aristotle meant when he declared that 'the roots of education are bitter but the fruits are sweet'.

Seamus undertook an interdisciplinary teaching programme and received a PGCEA, which entitled him to work as a nurse teacher. He remembers his teachers: Professor David James on educational psychology; Peter Jarvis on the sociology of education; and John Heron and his now famous six-category interventional analysis as important influences and as very positive role models in his early career.

Seamus was the first psychiatric nurse to receive a PhD from an Irish university. Seamus's PhD compared the learning approaches and experiences of student nurses in Northern Ireland and the Republic of Ireland. Nursing in Northern Ireland had just entered a linked university-based programme (Project 2000), whilst the

Republic still had apprenticeship-style training for nurses. His work was very appropriate as it was around this period that the nursing profession in the Republic of Ireland was beginning to evaluate and review alternative models of nurse education.

Later in his career Seamus, spent one week with Patricia Benner, when she received a Fellowship of the RCSI prior to her retirement. She had such insight and was deeply reflective on her career contributions. She was, as she wrote, about humility, humaneness and caring and, in Seamus' opinion, there was much more to her than just the writings.

MAJOR LIFE EVENTS

Seamus recalls one of the most significant personal events in his life as the death of his 19-year-old daughter, Natasha. She had a disability and was sick for many years with many episodes of hospitalisation. During this period, he gained deep insights into the wisdom and integrity of caring nurses, something one has to experience in order to understand. Seamus maintains that the role of informal carers in health services is very important and one that should be embraced in planning the future for nursing.

CONTRIBUTION TO NURSING

Seamus holds a joint appointment between the Nursing School and the Medical School at the RCSI. This ensures opportunities for interdisciplinary work. In the 200-year history of the RCSI, he became the first Professor of Nursing there in 1998. Having planned, developed and directed the School of Nursing & Midwifery, RCSI Bahrain, he continues to support developments there.

He states that his contributions to nursing are difficult for him to say but for others to judge. However, he highlights his contribution to the new era of university-based nursing and the undergraduate programme. While working as an education officer at An Bord Altranais, he authored the consultative documents on nursing education and the report on the future of nurse education and training in Ireland (1991, 1994), which subsequently helped in the commencement of an undergraduate education programme for nurses in Ireland. Thus, he had a role to play in the development of nurse education and, as a member of national committees, contributed to where nursing education in Ireland is today.

In 1992, he received an International Council of Nurses Award and in 2010 was selected as the national candidate for the International Fellowship Programme, awarded in recognition of outstanding professional achievements – his contributions to the improvement of nursing at national and international level. He also became the first nurse from the Republic of Ireland to be accepted into the prestigious American Academy of Nursing (AAN). Scholarship, leadership and innovations within nursing and health care at national and international level were part of the selection process.

From a professional perspective, with faculty colleagues in RCSI, he directed the development of the first suite of clinical nursing specialist postgraduate programmes incorporating a core curriculum. Seamus devised the first national programmes in many areas, most notably Infection Control and Wound Management. Also, under his stewardship, RCSI provided one of the first Nurse & Midwife Prescribing Programmes in Ireland and the first Sexual Assault/Forensic Nurse Examiners education programme.

Seamus has extensive international experience. He has supported the Ministry of Health in Saudi Arabia in establishing and monitoring a renal nursing programme. He also has developed and provided the first MSc in Nursing programme in the Kingdom of Bahrain.

Over the years, he has remained an advocate for psychiatric nursing and is currently an executive board member of the European Violence in Psychiatry Research Group. He has spoken at many mental health conferences on this topic and always will remain true to psychiatric nursing. He is currently primary investigator of a major European Union study on violence management across 17 countries, translated into 13 languages.

He is modest when he states that he has shown some leadership. He has led the education agenda in Ireland with others like

Professor Geraldine McCarthy.[2] He has been Principal Investigator on many research projects. He has achieved a grant income of over €3 million and his publications include over 120 journal papers, 12 books/book chapters and 14 national reports.

Seamus is currently the Principal Investigator with a research team that includes surgeons, anaesthetists, economists, and administrators on a Health Research Board-funded study to establish standards for day surgery in Ireland. He highlights the importance of interdisciplinary research and believes that nurses and midwives must have the confidence to lead in this area. He believes that his eight years spent with An Bord Altranais as an education officer provided him with deep insights into regulation and professionalism and how statutory systems work.

VISION FOR YOUR LIFE'S WORK

He is very passionate about European affairs and about European nursing and has published in the area. He believes in the important trend going forward through Europe where there will be unified systems in nursing in terms of how standards are approached and movement and collaboration acknowledged. He recognises the significant part that Europe will play in nursing into the future. He believes that there needs to be further effort in building the European Union (EU) agenda beyond the mandatory requirement of fulfilling EU Nursing Directives. More education collaboration and stronger nursing research agendas must be pursued through a European model.

COMPETENCIES, STRENGTHS AND VALUES

Seamus always aims to complete any tasks that he engages in; he aims to be fair, creative and enterprising and to be solution-orientated. He values caring nurses. People who are poor communicators, not good team players, who are inconsiderate of

---

[2]   **Chapter 15**, *Leadership in Action: Influential Irish Women Nurses' Contribution to Society*, Geraldine McCarthy & Joyce J. Fitzpatrick, Oak Tree Press, 2012.

others and tough on their juniors, are not valued by Seamus. He believes that tolerance is important and also the development of coping mechanisms. He sometimes sees early career academics getting frustrated and suggests that it is important at times to stand back, step outside and look in.

SIGNIFICANT CHALLENGES

One of the biggest challenges in nursing, he believes, is moving from being a student nurse to a staff nurse. Nurses' professional life is directed and bound by statutory regulation and associated rules. Only the High Court can remove a name from the nurses register and becoming a nurse means that an individual must understand these factors.

Setting up an academic department was another challenge. Seamus has established two in his career: the School of Nursing at Dublin City University and the School of Nursing at the RCSI in Bahrain.

OPPORTUNITIES THAT ENHANCED SUCCESS

He believes that his varied experiences in many organisations and in different countries have enhanced his success. He did not stay in any one place for long. He asserts that he would not be where he is today if he had not had experience in England. He believes that there is a vast opportunity for people to learn through travelling and learning about different countries and cultures.

Seamus describes himself as a 'sceptical optimist': an optimist because passion in time can transform and sceptical because of a healthy disrespect for dogma. Throughout his career, he has had a passion for nursing developments and has worked tirelessly to make changes happen.

OBSTACLES ENCOUNTERED AND LESSONS LEARNED

He includes in the obstacles encountered in his lifetime the begrudgers, those with delusions of adequacy and bureaucratic systems. The lessons learnt are to ignore the begrudgers and to understand that there are no winners in such scenarios.

ADVICE TO ASPIRING LEADERS

He believes confidence and competence are the most important attributes in any individual professional and thus one must develop and maintain both of these attributes. He thinks nursing needs to embrace an entrepreneurial spirit to further develop the profession. One needs to be competent, to make sure to get the appropriate training and to have the necessary skills to hold a specific position. Be supportive of staff, be fair, and remember that each individual has their own career inspirations and ambitions. Do not underestimate the value of communication. Use multi-media and technology to assist with communications, but do not forget the human aspect of communications.

And finally Seamus contends that: "The greater danger for most of us is not that our aim is too high and we miss it, but that it is too low and we reach it" (Tom Peters, quoting Michelangelo).

CHAPTER 5
DECLAN DEVANE

Margaret M. Murphy

Carpe diem – Seize the day.

Declan Devane is a Professor of Midwifery at the National University of Ireland Galway (NUIG) (appointed in November 2011). A native of the West of Ireland, Declan was born in Castlebar, Co. Mayo and lived there for 18 years. He attended national school in Caramore and went to St. Colman's all-boys secondary school in Claremorris. Declan is the eldest of six children, five boys and one girl. The family moved to Galway in the late 1980s, at which time Declan had left home to attend NUIG. He holds BSc, MSc and PhD degrees from NUIG. Declan is the first Professor of Midwifery in Ireland. He believes his appointment is important because it sets a par between nursing and midwifery at professorial level.

EARLY INFLUENCES

Financial independence was the impetus for Declan to enter nursing, since student nurses were employees of the health service and received a salary immediately on entering training. Declan had a male cousin who was a nurse. He provided a positive role model. Declan admits that the short term goals of financial independence and employment prospects were a non-vocational way into nursing; however, this reflected the views of many nursing students of that era.

He started his nursing training as the only man among 49 women students. Within a few months, he began to enjoy it and very quickly saw nursing as a potential career. There were other men in nursing in Galway and the environment was supportive to male nursing students. Declan credits his nursing tutors, who were very supportive of him as a man in nursing. In the clinical area, Declan noticed that some of the ward managers did treat him differently. He felt he was afforded a little more respect because of his gender but often was allocated to the heavier ward duties. He never noticed any reaction from the public that would have made him think that his gender was an issue in nursing though there was often an assumption from the public that he was a physician. However, he always wore his name badge and always introduced himself as a nurse, which clarified the situation quickly. Declan believes that, when it comes to caring, gender does not matter.

During his training, Declan felt well-supported by his family, particularly his maternal grandmother, and his student nursing group. He remains close to them to this day and believes he made lifelong friends. He believes that students are a fundamental social support for each other. When Declan qualified in nursing, permanent posts were scarce and he gained valuable experience as a staff nurse on the medical wards. At this time, Declan met his future wife, Marcella, one of his 49 nursing colleagues.

In 1992, Declan and Marcella began to seriously consider career options. In Ireland, to advance your career, three qualifications were desirable: general nursing, midwifery, and management. There was major uncertainty securing permanent work, and wishing to advance his career he set about applying for places on postgraduate midwifery programmes. Both Marcella and Declan secured places in Bristol to commence midwifery training.

Declan recognised from the outset that midwifery would be the career for him. He identified that midwifery had a boundary and a defined sphere of practice. The autonomy of midwifery practice, which led to great job satisfaction, also appealed to him. Upon qualification, Declan worked for four years on labour wards in Gloucestershire and Bristol. In 1998, Declan and Marcella moved back to Ireland and secured permanent midwifery posts in Dublin. Declan had completed his BSc in Nursing during this time in the United Kingdom (UK).

When reflecting on his achievements to date, Declan cites Marcella as his greatest supporter, his staunchest ally and his fiercest defender. According to Declan, her support was paramount in facilitating him in his professional career.

MAJOR LIFE EVENTS

Declan worked clinically in midwifery for two years upon his return to Ireland, before securing a job in midwifery education. He secured a permanent lectureship post in Trinity College Dublin in 2001, having completed an MSc degree. Then there was a research post, working to support the implementation and evaluation of the pilot midwifery-led units in the North East of the country. He worked on that project, securing a Health Research Board grant of €250,000 and completed his PhD. Declan cites this project as a major point in his career that opened up many opportunities. He became chair of the regional clinical practice guidelines group, developed project management skills, engaged with obstetric colleagues, management colleagues, and senior midwifery colleagues, and managed the capital development project. Upon completion of the project in 2008, he moved to Galway to take up a Senior Lecturer post in Midwifery at NUIG.

Declan considers himself extraordinarily fortunate with the people he has met and collaborated with over the years. He has known and worked with Professor Cecily Begley[3] for 15 years. They have a very strong relationship and still work very closely on many maternity care-related research projects and publications. Declan also has worked extensively with Professor Mike Clarke and the Cochrane collaboration and contributed widely to the Cochrane Library by producing Cochrane reviews on various maternity-specific topics.

During his time in the North Eastern Health Board, Declan had the opportunity to meet some wonderful midwifery colleagues and Health Board managers. At the time, the midwifery service was in the media spotlight due to the activities of Dr Michael Neary. Staff were supportive of change and wanted to make a difference. In the midwifery services, the success in the North East was due to the commitment of a large number of people from different areas of midwifery, obstetrics, and management and that was hugely important. When times became difficult and there were challenges, the group would refer back to the philosophy of midwifery care previously agreed upon.

VISION FOR YOUR LIFE'S WORK

Declan believes that there is a disconnect between what midwives are taught theoretically and what they are exposed to in clinical practice. Declan cites the medical profession, which has negotiated joint appointments between the university setting and the clinical practice setting with dedicated sessions for both. He wishes his own appointment attracted dedicated clinical sessions. To effect change in this area would require a vision from both the university sector and the Health Service Executive (HSE). He believes that, if the HSE was to pay for the clinical sessions, the universities could recruit additional staff and the health service would get the benefit of somebody very credible who has a lot to share. In this way, small

---

[3]   **Chapter 5**, *Leadership in Action: Influential Irish Women Nurses' Contribution to Society*, Geraldine McCarthy & Joyce J. Fitzpatrick, Oak Tree Press, 2012.

changes in the clinical practice area could be affected. Declan believes this would be something that could make a huge impact in supporting clinical colleagues in implementing change. This is one way he envisages that academia could influence clinical practice.

Declan also speaks strongly of the need for midwives to nurture and develop the profession through its newest entrants. He thinks that the re-orientation of maternity services will require high calibre graduate midwives. He believes the greatest strength of the current programme is the internship, built on the traditional apprentice training model, and for him this reinforces that the apprentice training model still has a very important role to play.

SIGNIFICANT CHALLENGES

Declan faced his greatest challenge two years ago when he and Marcella suffered the unimaginable loss of their beloved two-year-old son, Killian, while Marcella was pregnant with their second son. Understandably, Declan identifies this as a defining moment in their lives.

From a professional perspective, Declan's first exposure to the Irish maternity services surprised him and was the most difficult career transition he had to make. The role of midwife in Ireland was very different to what he was accustomed to in the UK. Though the cohorts of women were the same, the models of maternity care were starkly different and the biggest shock was the lack of any real midwifery autonomy. This was due to the dominant role of obstetrics in the care of normal pregnancy and birth in Ireland, despite the fact that the legislation that governs the activities of a midwife is identical in Ireland and the UK. While wishing to challenge and change its practices, Declan identified that the greatest obstacles often came from members of his own profession. Though he was supported by many managers and midwives, it was often from within the midwifery profession that Declan faced the staunchest opposition to his efforts to challenge the *status quo*. There was a culture clash between his experiences of the role of the midwife and the Irish midwives' experiences and, within that interface, things at some points were very difficult. To

overcome these challenges, Declan looked to the research evidence
and to his experiences from the UK to inform his clinical practice.

Declan identified another big challenge as the invisibility of
midwifery within the Irish maternity service and the wider public
arena. He recognised the need for midwives to understand and
distinguish the true role of the midwife and to translate it from the
classroom (where it was taught) into the clinical practice arena.
When this is achieved, midwives are able to educate the public and
other health care professionals on their roles and responsibilities.
His advice to midwives is clear: education and unity. The best
evidence on interventions in maternity care is available and
midwives have an obligation to provide care based on that
evidence. He cites the example of continued electronic foetal
monitoring of low risk women, despite the known risks of
increasing their chance of caesarean section by 20%. Declan believes
that some of the interventions that midwives do are perceived by
them as innocuous, innocent or without harm, but in actual fact
they can add harm.

Indeed, Declan believes that policy-makers need to change
policy, as having the majority of women cared for under the
medical model does not make clinical, economic or social sense.
Declan sees his role as trying to get this key issue in midwifery on
the national agenda and to establish a shift in thinking. He believes
that Ireland has a relatively small obstetric workforce in
comparison to other Organization for Economic Co-operation and
Development (OECD) countries and has relatively few
obstetricians providing care to 70,000 plus women per year. Yet
obstetricians continue to provide care to low risk women who do
not need their specialised care. He is working with the National
Midwifery Network, examining and reviewing guidelines that are
being produced by the HSE. There is very good international and
Irish evidence demonstrating categorically that midwife models of
care are safe, women prefer them and they are cost-effective.
Declan feels that, ultimately, the decision to re-orientate maternity
services away from the acute hospital sector is a political one, while
there is a myriad of evidence to support such a reorientation.
Declan hopes that he and others can use their positions to influence
policy. He is optimistic that change is on the horizon and cites a

maternity summit in Dublin early in 2012 where there were representatives from all maternity units in the country. Present were both obstetricians and midwives and it was the first time that he had seen such a gathering where the conversations were about maternity care policy. Declan believes that there was a recognition at that conference that there was a strong role for midwifery care. Women's groups – for example, the Association for the Improvement in Maternity Services (Ireland) – also are campaigning for changes in maternity care services. Declan believes that midwives need to embrace that movement and support it rather than view it as something threatening. Women are midwives' greatest allies in re-orientating Irish maternity services. Declan firmly believes in the absolute need for a professional, non-union organisation for midwifery, especially if a midwifery view on a particular maternity care issue is required.

ADVICE TO ASPIRING LEADERS

The leader is important to any movement but more important than the leader are the followers. These are the ones who develop the critical mass in terms of affecting change and encouraging others to participate. The key issue for leaders is to support each other in a similar manner to medical colleagues, who have a well-established history of peer-support. Communication skills are also vitally important in engaging with others; this is especially true with those who do not share your perspective. Declan believes that, while there is mutual respect between members of the multidisciplinary team, midwives' voices have not been to the forefront in developing the maternity care agenda.

His advice is to value the small and important things in life, count every blessing, and learn to recognise and prioritise what is truly important in life. Family and health should never be sacrificed for professional life, as it can only lead to regrets. He recommends that one reflects on 'Carpe diem' (Seize the day); professional opportunities that may present themselves need to be identified as such and taken. Friendships and networks need to be nurtured and built along the way, as they too provide valuable sources of support when needed.

Finally, Declan acknowledges that, though much of his success is due to hard work and the deliberate decisions he has taken, he also has been quite fortunate and lucky in the experiences he has had and with the people he has had the pleasure of knowing.

CHAPTER 6
LIAM DORAN

Josephine Hegarty

*You can – you have – great potential, and you can make a
difference. Now go and get on your journey.*

Liam Doran completed his training to become a Registered Mental
Handicap Nurse in St. John of God Hospital in St. Mary's, Drumcar
in Co. Louth. He subsequently completed an 18-month General
Nursing Programme in Our Lady of Lourdes Hospital in
Drogheda. During his student years, Liam was an active member of
the Irish Nurses Organisation (INO). Liam joined the INO, as

Student Officer, in June 1983 and subsequently worked as an Industrial Relations Officer and Deputy General Secretary before his appointment to the post of General Secretary in October 1998. Liam has completed a BA in Health Administration and a MA in Human Resource Management & Industrial Relations. In his role as General Secretary of the Irish Nurses & Midwives Organisation (INMO), Liam has taken the role of the lead negotiator in national negotiations relating to the pay, conditions and the roles that nurses and midwives assume within the Irish health services.

Liam is married to Patricia and he has two children, Adam and Aoife. When away from work, his main interests are his family, sport in general and in particular golf.

EARLY INFLUENCES

Liam Doran, an only child, spent much of his earlier life in England; his parents were forced to emigrate in the early 1960s to seek work. Liam grew up as part of the wider Irish community resident in England at the time. Although both his parents worked, the family would decamp to Ireland for the school summer holidays each year, much to Liam's enjoyment. When the economy in Ireland improved in the early 1970s, Liam's dad secured a job in Kilkenny and the Doran family returned to Ireland in 1974, after Liam completed his A levels.

In terms of Liam's wider family network, there were many nurses in his family which gave Liam "a good nursing perspective", and "nursing was in the blood" of his extended family. This, taken together with Liam's prior work with children with intellectual disabilities in England, fostered his interest in the caring professions. Liam noted that, from a personal perspective, he had always felt an innate sense inside himself that he wanted to care for those who were less able to care for themselves. In 1975, Liam began the process of applying for a place on an intellectual disability nursing programme, which at the time entailed writing to every single training school individually. He acquired a place on a nursing programme in St. John of God in St. Mary's, Drumcar in Co. Louth. However, Liam could not take up the offer of the place on the programme at the time, as he was hospitalised.

During this time, Liam had become proficient at golfing, with some success in various amateur competitions. Liam was offered the chance to make the transition to becoming a professional golfer in England in summer 1975. He spent 18 months as a professional golfer based in Canterbury Golf Club, Kent. He played golf for a living, taught golf and ran a golf shop at the golf club. However, Liam came to the realisation that, while he was good at golf, he felt he was not quite the calibre to make it in long-term professional golf. This, coupled with his yearning to return to Ireland and his continued interest in nursing as a potential career option, encouraged him to re-apply to St. John of God in St. Mary's, Drumcar for a place on the Mental Handicap Nursing programme (as it was termed at the time). He vividly remembers receiving a telegram confirming his place on the programme with a commencement date of 16 November 1976.

Liam remembers with fondness his three-year nursing programme. He treasures the memory of the clinical placement schedule, the rosters, the daily routines, extra-curricular visits, the clients and so on that was wrapped up in working in St. Mary's, Drumcar. Coincidentally, the Special Olympics movement was in its infancy around this time and Liam's first-ever radio interview was on Radio Carousel, based in Dundalk, to promote the Special Olympics Leinster Regional event that was taking place in Gormanston, at which some of the clients from St. Mary's were participating. At this early stage of his nursing career, a number of individuals, including Bridget O'Neill (known as Breege), Mary Cotter and Mary Coyne, helped to consolidate his belief that one could make a positive difference by being a registered nurse in intellectual disability.

While in Drumcar, Liam also met Patricia, who became his wife in 1981. After completing his nursing programme, Liam worked in St. Mary's as a Staff Nurse under the stewardship of the Director of Nursing, Ms Catherine Shine. In November 1980, Ms Shine summoned Liam to her office. Thinking that he had done something wrong, Liam was surprised by her offer of a secondment to take up a place on the postgraduate general nursing programme in Our Lady of Lourdes Hospital, Drogheda. Having consulted with Patricia, and considered the financial implications of dropping his salary, Liam decided to take up the offer on the 18-month programme. He had the distinction of being the second postgraduate male student in Our Lady of Lourdes Hospital. At the time, male students were not allowed to nurse female patients and they did not work on the female wards. Liam recalls that, for his final nursing exams, ironically there was a question on the post-operative care of a woman after a mastectomy.

While in Our Lady of Lourdes Hospital, Liam was positively influenced by a number of nurses, principally Kathleen Veale and Barbara Kennedy. Kathleen Veale, the Director of Nursing, challenged nurses to be the best they could be. Barbara (Babs) Kennedy was the ward sister in the male surgical ward. Liam described Babs as a great motivator, challenger, and leader. She expected all nurses to be fully informed.

After completing the general nursing programme, Liam gained experience in the Emergency Department. This period of time coincided with a relapse in the country's economic situation and was associated with a reduction in the number of nursing posts available. Liam returned to St. John of God in Drumcar to work in the Challenging Behaviour Unit (St. Raphael's).

During his student years both in Drumcar and Drogheda, Liam was involved in the Irish Nurses Organisation (INO) as a student representative. In the spring of 1983, the INO advertised for its first-ever student officer. Having given great thought to the potential offered by such an appointment, Liam interviewed for and was successful in obtaining the position. Liam started in the INO as the Student Officer on 13 June 1983. His first few years as the Student Officer were spent recruiting students, trying to build an infrastructure (a new student section), organising student seminars and ensuring that students felt a sense of belonging to the INO. Over the next five years, Liam worked in various capacities within the INO: Student Officer; Local Industrial Liaison Officer (greater Dublin area); Co-ordinator of Industrial Relations Activities (1992); Deputy General Secretary (1995); and, ultimately, General Secretary in October 1998. All these appointments were subject to open advertisement/ competition and Liam noted that he worked in apprenticeship in the rank immediately below that which he moved into.

Two factors were very important in terms of Liam's time within the INO: the people (the INO team) and the environmental context of the deteriorating country's fiscal situation and the associated cutbacks within the health services during the 1980s. The team within the INO provided guidance for Liam for his progression within the organisation. Ina Meehan (former General Secretary) was a lady who commanded great respect for her tremendous competence and incredible vision.

After Ina Meehan retired in 1996, the INO was faced with its greatest challenge: to remain as a conservative entity or to transform into a more transparent, assertive and visible organisation with a strong industrial relations presence. Given the backdrop of ward and hospital closures, redundancies, relocations and redeployments in the late 1980s and early 1990s, the organisation had to evolve out of necessity.

This period of major cuts in the health services was associated with unease with the role, status and remuneration of nursing's clinical work force. Liam became the Deputy General Secretary in 1995, coinciding with a period of major industrial unrest. Minister for Health, Michael Noonan, when faced with the prospect of an all-out national industrial action on the part of nurses and midwives, agreed that there should be a major review of how nurses and midwives were viewed, their role and function within the health services, their career pathways and their education. A complete overview of nursing and midwifery – the Commission on Nursing, chaired by Ms. Justice Mella Carroll – in essence was the political response to the prospect of major disruption within the health services. Liam was very much a constant media presence during this time of unrest, articulating on the national airwaves the difficulties that nurses and midwives faced.

The Commission on Nursing reported in September 1998, with 200 recommendations. It is Liam's belief that the nine days of industrial unrest in 1999 consolidated from a political perspective the need to implement these recommendations, which has been done.

VISION FOR YOUR LIFE'S WORK

When asked to consider his work to date, Liam placed emphasis on the 10 years from 1996 to 2006 and the changes that have taken place in Ireland in terms of the clinical status and academic preparation of nurses and midwives. He noted that no other country within the Organization for Economic Co-operation and Development (OECD) could come close to replicating the pace of change that has been seen in Ireland in that 10-year period, particularly as nurse and midwifery undergraduate education has moved from an apprenticeship model to a university-based BSc honours degree, including an internship clinical placement. This was one of the most positive achievements of that 10-year journey for Liam and the INO.

Liam wished to acknowledge the role of representative bodies as being the catalyst for what happened in the late 1990s and early 2000s. These representative bodies (and Liam as one of their representatives) were able to channel the pent-up frustration of nurses, midwives and the nursing community to create a platform for massive change. This is one of the successes that Liam is most proud of.

COMPETENCIES, STRENGTHS AND VALUES

A belief in what one is doing is crucial to effect change, according to Liam Doran, and one needs to believe that what one is advocating for is a better alternative. In addition, to provide leadership, it is important to believe that one is doing the right thing, while placing emphasis on the core values of inner integrity and honesty. To listen to and remain in touch with the reality of clinical practice and the constituents one represents is important. It is also important to value the key role of these front-line staff within the health services.

In addition, to achieve change, one has to have the ability to work the media. The modern world has a very short memory, thus the importance of a clear sound-bite in a way that the media wants to listen to and to use. Liam notes that one of his advantages is that he has honed the ability to relate to the media in a way that conveys his message clearly.

CHARACTERISTICS OF LEADERS

Liam noted the importance of self-belief, belief in the profession and integrity. One needs to be confident and be honest with oneself and believe that nursing and midwifery can make a difference to people who are sick and to people who are in challenging situations.

SIGNIFICANT CHALLENGES

Liam describes 18 October 1999 as one of the loneliest days of his life. He recalls waking up in a hotel in Dublin and hearing the 6 o'clock news headlines. The first item on the news was that 40,000 nurses were going on a continuous dispute – their first-ever national strike at 8 o'clock the following morning. Liam was 12 months in the post of General Secretary. He believes he could not have survived without first having done his 'homework' internally within the organisation (knowing what the organisation and its members wanted) and, second, having a great team around him. Third, Liam believes that one needs to be passionate about one's beliefs if one is to overcome the challenges. Liam makes no apologies for being absolutely unequivocal about being a spokesperson or an advocate for that. He notes that, while trying to be the leader of the INMO, in that regard it is about advocating for the nurse and midwife, it is not *per se* about maximising the visibility of nursing or midwifery or maximising the income that comes with it. He feels he has tried his best to ensure that the Irish public health system is absolutely capable of delivering the best possible patient outcomes and he is adamant that, for that to happen the registered nurse or the registered midwife has to be given the authority, the responsibility, the accountability to deliver the best possible outcomes for patients.

OBSTACLES ENCOUNTERED AND LESSONS LEARNED

One of the major obstacles to effecting change that Liam has encountered is that, in his view, many people in positions of authority, whether in political establishments, the civil service or higher management in the health service, simply do not see nurses or midwives as true professionals. They still see them as people providing a relatively low level of interaction with a sick or challenged person and they do not afford nurses and midwives the respect that other health professionals would have assigned to them automatically. For Liam, this factor alone has been the biggest obstacle that has slowed down the pace of progress and obstructed it.

The second major obstacle to effecting change is the cost of providing a nursing and midwifery service. The reality is that nurses and midwives are expensive, not in the sense that the individual nurse is expensive, but when one considers that nursing personnel comprise 35% of the total health workforce, then by definition they are an expensive element within the service. So the system goes after cutbacks in nursing much faster because greater savings can be made more quickly using this *modus operandi*. His overriding concern is that such savings ultimately lead to a down-skilling of the skill mix so as to save money.

In terms of lessons learned, Liam notes that, during the various periods of industrial unrest, many different organisations and individuals sharing a common cause, a common agenda, were required to push it mutually from their different perspectives in order to realise a new place, a better place, for nursing and midwifery. A great team, both to anticipate and to overcome challenges, thus is important.

ADVICE TO ASPIRING LEADERS

Liam gives the same advice he recollects Ms. Shine (Assistant Director of Nursing, 1980) giving to him, "You can – you have – great potential, you can make a difference. Now, go and get on your journey".

As a leader, Ina Meehan commanded tremendous respect; she had a tremendous aurora of professionalism about her. As a leader, you must be willing to allow individuals to develop leadership potential and carve out a new identity, build a great team, take incremental steps required to effect change, and see goals achieved.

CHAPTER 7
GERARD FEALY

Doman Al-Omari

*Know when to be silent because silence is influencing
in many ways.*

Gerard Fealy is Professor of Nursing and Associate Dean for Research & Innovation at the School of Nursing, Midwifery & Health Systems, at University College Dublin (UCD). He was born in Monaghan into a farming family and is the second of five children. He has one older sister and three younger brothers. He is one of the leading professionals in historical research in nursing in

Ireland. He completed a Bachelor of Nursing (1989) and a Master's in Education (1995). He obtained his PhD (2003) from the School of Education at UCD. He has several publications, including authored books, chapters in collaborative books, articles in peer-reviewed journals, conference publications and reports. He has a leading position in the field of historical research, and has made a strong contribution to nursing education and clinical practice.

EARLY INFLUENCES

Gerard commenced his nursing training in 1975 by undertaking a traditional nursing certificate programme in psychiatric nursing at St. Patrick's Hospital in Dublin. In 1980, he began his general nurse training at St. James's Hospital in Dublin, where he stayed for over 15 years. He also trained as a coronary care nurse in Dublin in 1984.

As a child, he was influenced by his parents, especially his father, who worked as a farmer. His father taught him always to do the right thing, and encouraged him to work hard, be a good person and live a good life. Because of his position between his sister and his brothers in a small family, he was influenced by them also, especially by his older sister.

Outside his family, Gerard was influenced by one of his schoolteachers, who had a different style of teaching from the other teachers. He used to talk about things that were outside the school curriculum, such as the world in general and also about politics. That teacher had a positive influence on Gerard in a way that Gerard cannot explain.

Throughout his nursing training and career, Gerard was influenced by his nursing tutors in psychiatric and general training. Furthermore, Gerard cites his current Head of School (Martin McNamara) as a strong leader who has had a strong positive influence on him. Ann Marie Rafferty has been influential because of her writing as a historian. Siobhan Nelson in Toronto and Professor Roger Watson have influenced Gerard with their well-formulated arguments and their ability to truly profess nursing through their work.

Other influences on Gerard include his first Matron (Director of Nursing), Ms Kelly. She was a traditional matron in every sense, but he respected her standards of care.

Over the past 10 years, Gerard says he has been particularly influenced by Julie Fairman, Pat Antonio and Arleen Keeling. These writers are nurse historians, and have been leading the field of nursing history research for many years and thus influenced him in his chosen research field.

MAJOR LIFE EVENTS

A major life event was obtaining his first nursing qualification. This was a great achievement, considering that he came from a small rural background where most of his contemporaries from school would not have gone to college and certainly would not have attended higher education. Instead, they worked in labouring jobs in building, trading and farming. His achievements in nursing made him one of only a few men in nursing at that time.

The next major positive event in Gerard's life was achieving his doctorate degree. Achieving promotions to Senior Lecturer and Associate Professor were also major life events.

In Gerard's personal life, getting married and the birth of his two children were defining life events.

The major negative life events were the death of his father, mother, and father in-law within a period of 18 months in the 1980s.

CONTRIBUTION TO NURSING

Gerard has made multiple contributions to nursing, including the clinical work he carried out early in his professional life, particularly his work in the coronary care unit.

In his professional career, Gerard has spent more time in education and research than in the other aspects of nursing. As a Principal Tutor in Our Lady of Lourdes Hospital, Drogheda, he was responsible for shaping the first nursing curriculum for the Diploma in Nursing, which was affiliated with Dundalk Institute of Technology. Gerard also had a major input into the introduction of the BSc degree programmes at UCD in 1994. Another major contribution was in shaping the nursing experience and nursing practice elements of the curriculum. He believes that his own doctoral thesis and his associated published work have contributed to aspects of nursing history that had not been detailed before. His scholarship in the field of historical research has made a contribution to the advancement of nursing because, in his opinion, there are a limited number of people, nationally and internationally, interested in this kind of research. Gerard hopes that this work will remain important for scholars for many years to come.

In higher education, Gerard supervises doctorate students, another important contribution to nursing's future.

VISION FOR YOUR LIFE'S WORK

His vision for the future of his work is to continue developing nursing as a discipline in the universities, particularly through research and teaching, and also through developing the subject of nursing through scholarship. He hopes that, by the time he retires, the graduate nursing students of recent years will be capable and successful leaders.

Gerard's vision for the future is for nursing practice and nursing research to come closer through evidence-based practice, and by holding substantive dialogue between areas of nursing practice and educational institutions on a regular basis. Gerard would like to see certain aspects of nursing scholarship become more firmly established by encouraging clinical nursing research where the aspects of practice are tested, which equates to 'more research on how we nurse rather than how we think we nurse'.

COMPETENCIES, STRENGTHS AND VALUES

Gerard believes that he has a reputation for being competent, particularly in writing, which he has developed over time. Also, he has good communication skills, is a good administrator, and can organise, plan, and manage.

Gerard's strengths include his persistence and his ability to finish tasks. If he starts a project, he takes responsibility to see it through. He can do things with a sense of humour, but this does not affect the seriousness of his work. He goes through life with an outlook of the glass being half-full rather than half-empty.

Gerard has a strong work ethic and he is loyal to his institution, his employer, his colleagues and his family. He maintains that loyalty is an important strength. He also believes that maintaining friendship is important. Other values that Gerard holds to be important are the values of truth and family, particularly being a good parent and husband.

CHARACTERISTICS OF LEADERS

Gerard has strong views about what constitutes a good leader. Leaders need to be knowledgeable about their field, should 'walk the walk' before their followers, and have the ability to see the perspectives of followers without compromising their own position as the leader.

Leaders also have to be able to communicate their vision to others through their actions. In order to lead a group in an organisation, one must know the goals of the organisation and the ability of individuals.

He believes that being a good researcher and educator emerges from the practice of good teaching, researching and writing.

SIGNIFICANT CHALLENGES

Gerard names a number of challenges faced as a leader, such as persuading people to share his vision of how students should learn, how we should train nurses in a more generic sense, and how to conduct research.

One major challenge expressed by Gerard is day-to-day interaction with people, as people can misinterpret intentions and often you can misinterpret theirs. Furthermore, people may not share your vision, or they even may want to destroy your vision.

Internal motivation is a challenge, especially when you are trying hard over a long period of time to do something. Extrinsic motivation, such as the speed of knowledge and the constant dynamic of change, also presents challenges. The nursing degree programme has been running for the last 10 years, and though it seems established, there is a challenge in re-evaluating it and perhaps re-inventing it.

OPPORTUNITIES THAT ENHANCED SUCCESS

Gerard likes to think that he made his own success in life. The opportunity to enter a degree course in 1986 was an opportunity created by others, but Gerard took it. Another opportunity was starting his doctorate degree after he became an academic, as he was in the right environment. And another opportunity was being one of the first academics in UCD's School of Nursing, which meant that he was able to place himself in a position of leadership that ultimately led to success. The financial situation in the country in the late 1990s meant it was a good time for introducing nursing into the university system. Gerard was there when it happened, so was able to gain a position in the university and thus to influence education and research.

OBSTACLES ENCOUNTERED AND LESSONS LEARNED

Gerard stated that the main obstacle to any leader is people, as it is people who create structures and people who can change them.

Gerard feels he has learnt many lessons throughout his life. For example, he has learned how to be self-reliant and how to identify people that can be relied on. These are people who are allies to your goals and who share your vision. He believes it is important to take opportunities when they present themselves, while taking care not to jump in too quickly without first weighing positives and negatives.

ADVICE TO ASPIRING LEADERS

Leaders should focus on projects they believe in, reach goals, be aware that there are power-brokers, and be alert to the systems used. Use the power well, for advancing the discipline of nursing and ultimately advancing the care that patients receive.

Leaders must be visible, and their influence should carry on through what they write. Leaders should speak up for their discipline, but should also know when to be silent because silence is influential in many ways. Leaders should act as role models.

CHAPTER 8
PAUL GALLAGHER

Anne Cleary

Adopt a 'can-do' approach, even in difficult times.

Paul Gallagher is Director of Nursing at St. James's Hospital, Dublin. He was born in Letterkenny, Co. Donegal and grew up in Mullingar, Co. Westmeath. He is one of five boys and the only one who chose nursing as a career. His eldest brother is a teacher, two other brothers are carpenters and the fourth is a chef. Both his parents are retired – his father, Fionn, retired as Director of Nursing from St. Loman's Hospital, Mullingar – but are very actively involved in the local community. From a young age, Paul knew he wanted to be a nurse. When growing up, he did not consider himself to be an excellent student; however, when introduced to nurse education, he excelled and qualified with a distinction in both Psychiatric Nursing and General Nursing.

EARLY INFLUENCES

In 1984, at the age of 18, Paul left Mullingar and began nurse training in psychiatry in St. Loman's Hospital in Palmerstown, Co. Dublin. He worked for eight months as a Staff Nurse in St. Loman's, before commencing his postgraduate general nurse training programme in Beaumont Hospital, Dublin. Paul began working in the Neurosurgical Intensive Care Unit (ICU) in Beaumont Hospital and subsequently completed a postgraduate course in neuroscience nursing. He worked for three years in this unit, where he gained substantial experience but felt he needed new challenges. He moved to New York, USA and worked in the Cardio-thoracic ICU at the Mount Sinai Medical Centre, Manhattan, New York, one of the oldest and largest teaching hospitals in the United States. Four years at Mount Sinai earned him valuable experience, working and living in one of the biggest cities in the world.

Aside from being anxious to return to Ireland, the main reason for returning home was to begin his Master's in Business Administration (MBA) in Health Service Management (Royal College of Surgeons in Ireland/University College Dublin). Paul found this programme of study very challenging and a huge personal commitment. The MBA, however, exposed him to multidisciplinary and interdisciplinary approaches, which he believes are very important in management. While completing the programme, he continued to work in the Neurosurgical ICU in Beaumont Hospital. On completion, Paul received his first nursing promotion and was appointed as Charge Nurse in the Neurosurgical ICU and subsequently to the position of Nursing Practice Development Co-ordinator. During this time, he applied for and was fortunate enough to be funded by Beaumont Hospital to pursue the Office of Health Management Millennium

Leadership Development Programme. The purpose of this programme was to develop the skills and competencies of managers to work with teams on specific challenges facing them in their health services organisations. These challenges related to improving internal management systems and processes and health service delivery. This educational programme involved many projects as well as action-based learning, which Paul felt was very beneficial to his development. It also allowed him to apply his learning from the MBA. Subsequently, Paul was appointed to the position of Assistant Director of Nursing in the surgical division in Beaumont. He remained in this position for five years and during this time he was sponsored by Johnson & Johnson to undertake a leadership programme in Fontainebleau, France. This was a multidisciplinary programme involving nurse managers, general hospital management, consultants and other health professionals.

Paul acknowledges his parents as having a major influence on him, both personally and professionally. Paul often asks his father for professional advice and support on current issues, as he has the knowledge and know-how and has experienced many difficulties in his own working life. Another major influence from his younger days was his father's mother, who showed great interest and enthusiasm. Even, at times, when he did not feel he had worked to the best of his ability, his grandmother continued to support him without judgement.

Paul was not sure what his career path would be, but he vividly recounts from a very young age being exposed to sick people. His grandmother had been unwell for some time and the impact of visiting the older person's facility in Mullingar had a profound impact on Paul. He recalled attending social events in St. Loman's Hospital, Mullingar and remembers being with the patients with mental health issues and having fun with them. Paul recognised early how he was exposed to people who were dependent on health care workers, and that influence alone was so important, because it guided him in terms of what he really wanted to do. This type of exposure set the scene and gave him a sense of responsibility.

He acknowledges his friend and colleague, Marie Keane, former Director of Nursing in Beaumont, who was a very positive influence. Ann Mulligan (Nurse Tutor), since deceased, is credited also by Paul as having had a significant impact on his early career.

The other influences in his life were the team of nurses he worked with in the Neurosurgical ICU, as they had fantastic enthusiasm and team spirit in the midst of caring for such a vulnerable patient group. Indeed, seven former members of the nursing team from the ICU have been appointed to Director of Nursing positions throughout the country. He believes his neurosurgical experience laid the foundation for the future because of the management and the style of leadership support demonstrated. It was a very motivating place to work. Staff were encouraged to progress and develop.

Paul also noted that his good friend and colleague, Suzanne Dempsey (Director of Nursing, Children's University Hospital, Temple Street), was another person who had a significant impact on his professional development. He believes that a good leader will be influential from a very early stage.

MAJOR LIFE EVENTS

One of his major life events was beginning nurse training. He knew from a very early stage that he wanted to be a nurse. He concentrated on nurses who were enthusiastic about their careers from a very early stage. Staff nurses who were not long qualified but had continued to develop themselves by continuing study were his role models. He completed a number of diploma programmes in the Royal College of Surgeons in Ireland in pursuit of lifelong and academic learning. He also saw this as beneficial for his *curriculum vitae*, as he had a genuine interest in progressing his career. Even though he chose to work in the intensive care environment after qualifying as a Registered General Nurse, he continues to use the skills learned in psychiatry frequently in general nursing.

He refers to being at the right place and at the right time when the Director of Nursing positions for St. James's Hospital, Dublin and Our Lady of Lourdes Hospital, Drogheda were advertised simultaneously. Marie Keane, his manager at the time, was very supportive of the two applications. He was successful in achieving both but chose the position in St. James's, which he has never regretted. It was his first exposure to the clinical directorate model of management and provided a steep learning curve during his first year as Director of Nursing.

St. James's Hospital prides itself as being the largest academic hospital in the country and Paul is responsible for almost 1,900 qualified nurses, student nurses and health care assistants. He acknowledges that he would be unable to do this work without the support of the Assistant Directors of Nursing. On taking up this position, he initially described his role as not unlike that of a sole trader. "You are the only person with that title in the hospital and everybody comes to you with their problems", he explained and this was a big challenge he had to overcome. Now he feels that he works very effectively with the team of Assistant Directors of Nursing and also as part of the wider corporate management team, led by the Chief Executive Officer. During challenging times, it is necessary to ensure that nursing is placed strategically on everybody's agenda. The position continues to present new challenges with less resources and sicker patients and, at the same time, one is expected to implement new ideas.

CONTRIBUTION TO NURSING

He continuously contributes to improving patient care and to making the experience of the patient as good as it can be, either the patient getting well or contributing to a patient's happy death. Paul does this with support of his team, whom he challenges while they equally challenge him. He reiterates that he could not be an effective Director of Nursing without the support of the nursing management team at St. James's.

Another contribution to nursing in general is his involvement in the Dublin Academic Teaching Hospitals Directors of Nursing Group (DATHs DONs). This is an important forum for networking with other Directors of Nursing to share experiences and work to improve and address the nursing agenda from a Dublin perspective.

He also contributes to the profession by being an active member of the Executive Council for the Irish Association of Directors of

Nursing & Midwifery (IADNAM) and is the association's Honorary Secretary. At Council, he can support and influence how nursing and midwifery leadership can contribute to and improve outcomes for patients, health care management and the health services at national level.

One of his early projects in St. James's was introducing Nurse Prescribing of Medicinal Products. This was a new venture for the profession and challenged nurses and physicians to introduce a significant change. Initially, it was difficult to get 'buy in' from some colleagues; however, there are now 18 Nurse Prescribers at St. James's. This was achieved by using a piecemeal approach to implement the initiative but a great deal of negotiation was required. St. James's is at the initial stages of introducing an Early Warning Scoring System for the patient, which will fulfil a requirement in terms of improved patient care and also assist the hospital in its preparation for accreditation later this year.

COMPETENCIES, STRENGTHS AND VALUES

Paul believes that honesty and integrity are essential in his role and he endeavours to instil these important values in others. These values and strengths were honed from an early age but also developed from working with more experienced people, people who mean well and have a positive attitude to their work and a strong work ethic. Another strength is that, despite being a corporate manager, the patient is always at the centre of care. Paul has to keep patient care on the agenda during difficult times, when others may not consider clinical issues as important.

CHARACTERISTICS OF LEADERS

The ability to communicate effectively with patients and families and to interact effectively with corporate management and senior decision-makers requires a wide range of communication skills. Being able to articulate the nursing and patient care agenda cannot be underestimated. Treating everyone as equal is vital, as is always leading by example and not losing sight of what is important.

SIGNIFICANT CHALLENGES

Paul is aware of many challenges but maintains that practice can change despite difficult financial times. Most recently, the greatest challenge has been the impact of the moratorium on staff recruitment. Skill mix is also a significant issue, with nursing staff being replaced with junior or less qualified staff or not being replaced at all. The challenge is to keep staff motivated and try to maintain quality patient care. Encouraging and supporting change is important. However, he credits St. James's staff with adopting a strong 'can do' approach, as there is a very strong and positive culture within the organisation.

He sees the need to improve nursing research, both nationally and internationally. He has established a Nursing Research Access Committee at St. James's, and the hospital convenes annual quality, audit and research seminars. He has obtained valuable funding from the National Council for the professional development of nursing and midwifery and from the Health Service Executive (January 2011) in support of introducing a Health Care Researcher to work with clinical nursing staff in developing nursing research and this role is supported by a joint research collaborative that Paul has established in partnership with the School of Nursing & Midwifery, Trinity College Dublin. There are now over 12 research projects at various stages of progress and a number are awaiting publication in peer-reviewed journals. He is determined to improve the nursing research profile of St. James's. As the Director of Nursing, he is acutely aware of the profile that the hospital has as one of the main players in the Irish health system and he continues to support nursing research in the hospital, with the ultimate goal of improving patient outcome.

ADVICE TO ASPIRING LEADERS

Be aware of the organisational culture; motivate staff at all levels; set realistic achievable goals so you do not suffer burnout; set the agenda with staff so they know what to expect; treat everyone with respect; adopt a 'can do' approach; and realise that there is always someone to support and mentor you to work effectively. Take up a new position for the right reasons and have a plan and a goal from early on in one's career. Be at the corporate table and represent the nursing profession and patient care agenda. Be involved with key players and network.

CHAPTER 9
JUSTIN GLEESON

Patricia Leahy-Warren

Good leaders develop through a never-ending process of self-study, education, training, and experience.

Justin Gleeson is employed by the HSE Addiction Service but maintains a clinical role for all substance-misusing women who present to the Rotunda Hospital for their maternity care. He undertook a Diploma in Nursing Studies at the National University of Ireland Galway (NUIG) (1999) and completed a BSc in Nursing Studies in NUIG (2000) and a Postgraduate Diploma in Midwifery from Trinity College Dublin (2003). Since then, he has undertaken many courses in the area of addiction and sexual health, including Certificates in Addiction Studies and Crisis Pregnancy Counselling from the National University of Ireland Maynooth.

EARLY INFLUENCES

Justin was born in Clarinbridge, Co. Galway, fifth in a large family of five sisters and two brothers. Justin's mother is a Registered Nurse but had discontinued working as a nurse before he was born. His father was an army officer, based in Galway and spent a lot of time in the Middle East, where they lived as a family from 1989 to 1990. During this time, Justin went to school in Israel as a young adolescent, which he believes was a very good experience as he matured a lot while living there and experiencing a very different culture. It was a very turbulent time in the Middle East and he and his family left on the eve of the invasion of Kuwait, which he described as 'absolute mayhem'. He believes that he experienced a lot of things that other 13- or 14-year-old boys never did.

The people in his family who influenced him greatly were his maternal grandfather and his mother. During his childhood, Justin spent time with his grandfather, who was a retired General Practitioner (GP). He came to visit regularly when his father was away and was a great support for Justin's mother, in trying to manage eight 'wild children' in the west of Ireland. Justin described him as a very quiet, kind and approachable man who had an ability to resolve situations by saying very little. They never attended a GP as children, as they were always looked after by their grandfather

His mother was born in Trent, United Kingdom and trained as a nurse in Guy's Hospital in London. She regularly visited her family in Clifden, where they owned Stanley's drapery shop, which is still there and is one of the oldest surviving businesses in the area. It was here that she met Justin's dad and they married and settled in Galway, where he was stationed with the Irish Army.

Justin's mother continued to work as a nurse until just before Justin was born. Although her formal employment stopped, she continued to practice as the unofficial district nurse, with relatives, neighbours and friends accessing her services for every ailment, bump and bruise. Justin greatly admired the level of respect she generated within their community and he continues to seek her opinion on issues affecting his own family before anyone else.

A major event in Justin's life that had an influence on him pursuing a career in nursing was being cared for by a male nurse in accident and emergency following a motorcycle accident when he was 16 years old. It was his first encounter with a male nurse and he pulled back the curtain to observe everything that was going on that night so he could see what the nurse was doing. On leaving the hospital that night, Justin was very sure about two things: that he would never drive a motorcycle again and that he would pursue a career in nursing.

MAJOR LIFE EVENTS

Justin was a student on the first group of Diploma in Nursing students in Ireland (1999) and went on to do his BSc almost immediately, while working during the weekends. He got a variety of clinical nursing experience and once graduated, he went travelling. While visiting a friend working in the Rotunda Hospital and walking around there, Justin felt it was a very different environment to that of a general hospital. Following this, he did an interview and received a place in the midwifery programme. He returned from his travels and was very unsettled, questioning whether he had made the right decision. He found the apprentice training very different from university training, as there were only 18 students as opposed to such large numbers in the Diploma programme.

Justin was very influenced by Declan Devane (now Professor of Midwifery at National University of Ireland Galway – see **Chapter 5**), who was a midwifery tutor, when he was having doubts about his decision to pursue a career in midwifery. By observing Declan interacting with women and gaining their trust, Justin learned from him. This helped Justin to focus on formulating an environment where the woman trusted him as her midwife rather than focusing on his gender as a barrier to her care. Justin was fortunate also that there was another male midwife within his class. They were a great support to each other as were his classmates, including his wife, whom he met for the first time on the course. They were a very close group who provided both psychological and academic support to each other.

He found midwifery training entirely different to nursing and, at times, a little bit intimidating. During this transitional period of uncertainty, he was struggling and very self-conscious of his gender inhibiting his ability to become a midwife. However, observing other male midwife role models like Colm O'Boyle and Declan Devane and their passion for midwifery inspired him to continue to strive to be a good midwife. He became more comfortable and confident in his ability as a midwife and was influenced also by others such as Louise Hanrahan and Joan Lawlor from Trinity College Dublin. Being a male midwife in Ireland is no longer unusual, as there are a number of them practicing now.

CONTRIBUTION TO NURSING

Justin teaches in University College Dublin, Trinity College Dublin, St. Munchin's Hospital in Limerick and also gives an education programme in Cork. He is planning to do a programme addressing substance misuse in pregnancy training for midwives in the Coombe Hospital, Dublin next year. He also teaches on the Certificate in Addiction Studies in Nursing programme and frequently works with the various Local Drug Task Forces throughout the country. He works in close collaboration with his Clinical Midwife Specialist (CMS) colleagues, Vickie Hurley in National Maternity Hospital, and Deirdre Carmody in the Coombe Hospital. He is working also with Our Lady of Lourdes Hospital in Drogheda, because a lot of the women who live in the North Dublin area would attend that hospital rather than coming into the city so they are seeing more and more women who are on methadone maintenance therapy or who are actively using illicit substances.

His brief is to work with women who primarily have an opiate addiction, with poly drug use, including benzodapazadines and stimulant drugs, such as cocaine and snow blow. Women who are alcoholics come under the remit of the psychiatric services but Justin hopes to address this in 2013, as it is the only known teratogen recreational drug that can cause serious consequences for the foetus. He believes there is a need for more formal training in relation to this subject for midwives and for women.

Currently, he has caseload of 60 rather than the recommended 40 women at any one time. Justin provides antenatal care for clients in the Rotunda and works as a member of the Danger of Viral Exposure (DOVE) clinical team. As these women have high-risk pregnancies, it is an obstetrician consultant-led service with other multidisciplinary staff, including social workers and an infectious disease specialist midwife.

He also visits his clients in the community, where he has built up a trusting relationship with them and they will attend there for their antenatal visits when they don't show for their hospital appointments.

COMPETENCIES, STRENGTHS AND VALUES

Justin has worked hard to develop and strengthen his communication skills, which he deems to be the core competency in working with vulnerable women. He believes these skills are not innate and are heavily influenced by the women he meets every day. Other strengths include being quite open and honest, empathetic and the belief that he is making a difference. He also believes a good sense of humour is vital to relieving tension as well as diffusing hostility. He describes effective leaders as "knowing how to use humour to energise followers" and suggests this is a vital asset in formulating relations in a group of vulnerable women where first impressions often last.

OTHER LEADERS WHO INFLUENCED YOU

Besides those Justin has mentioned already, one of the most influential midwives, who continues to have a major impact on his development, is his wife Charmaine. They were in the same class during their midwifery training and, although they were both competitive as students, they supported each other through the highs and lows of student and professional lives. Charmaine's passion for midwifery and constant striving for excellence, according to Justin, is "both personally and professionally infectious and inspiring".

Throughout his career, he has worked with midwives and managers from whom he has learned a great deal about being a leader. Their ability to communicate their vision to others was both uplifting and inspiring. Their effective leadership skills made others feel good about themselves as well as the work they were doing. At times of crisis, they were the ones who took charge, never panicked and generated a calm that ensured each staff member maintained their focus throughout such situations.

CHARACTERISTICS OF A LEADER

Justin describes good leaders as those who are passionate about what they do and channel their passion and enthusiasm to inspire others, as passion can be contagious. They need to believe in their ability to lead, as this self-confidence is an essential foundation to generate change. A good leader needs to be able to motivate people to believe in themselves and to strive always to do the best they can in everything they do. A good leader needs to instil trust in their followers, as this often gives them the courage to innovate, take risks and push themselves beyond their comfort zones to find success.

SIGNIFICANT CHALLENGES

In midwifery, Justin worked in the delivery suite, where in general the experiences were extreme levels of joy and happiness. This transition was even more difficult for Justin, as moving from an insular hospital structure to working on his own was very challenging. At first, he felt vulnerable and lonely but quickly started to form relationships in the community services and to build a service that centred on the needs of the women he cares for.

Justin also learned very quickly on his feet with regards to taking responsibility. He became a Clinical Midwife Manager within two years of qualifying as a midwife. He became a senior midwife almost overnight, taking over in charge of a labour ward with 20 to 25 deliveries a night. He felt confident and up to the challenge as he believed in his own abilities and learned from those around him. He ensured that he worked with midwives and managers whom he could gain from and avoided those who were negative. He recommends newly-qualified nurses and midwives to do the same.

OPPORTUNITIES THAT ENHANCED SUCCESS

Justin believes he was fortunate to have trained in nursing and midwifery when the professions were undergoing great change. There were plenty of opportunities for aspiring nurses and midwives who wanted to remain in clinical practice and use their expert skills to improve patient outcomes and contribute to health policy development. His early promotion increased his self-confidence. He was fortunate to have received support from experienced practitioners across all the professional groups he works with and also that he is accepted by the substance-misusing population.

OBSTACLES ENCOUNTERED AND LESSONS LEARNED

Justin believes that initially being a man in midwifery was perceived by him as an obstacle but, in hindsight, his young age and maturity may have been contributory factors. Working with, and having learnt from, those passionate about midwifery has obliterated those obstacles. He has found also that women are very accepting of male midwives, as it is not so much about the gender of the midwives as it is about their communication and empathy skills. Through his experiences and modification of various approaches, Justin now manages to deal with such situations by easing a woman's anxieties before they have a chance to develop.

ADVICE TO ASPIRING LEADERS

Justin believes good leaders are made, not born. They develop through a never-ending process of self-study, education, training, and experience. He believes that anyone can cultivate the proper leadership traits if they have the will to do so.

CHAPTER 10
BRIAN KEOGH

Omar Melhem

Good leaders should not be obsessed with power.

Brian Keogh was born in Dublin and is employed as a Lecturer in nursing at the School of Nursing & Midwifery, Trinity College Dublin (TCD). He was the only person in his family who studied nursing, and was not influenced by any of his family members before deciding to commence a nursing career. He completed a three-year Certificate in Psychiatric Nursing (1992); a Bachelor of Nursing Studies (BNS) from Dublin City University (DCU) (1998);

a Postgraduate Diploma in Further & Higher Education from University of Ulster (UU) (2000); a Postgraduate Diploma in Nurse Education from UU (2001); a MSc in Advanced Nursing from UU (2002); a Higher Diploma in Education from TCD (2004); a Postgraduate Diploma in Statistics from TCD (2004); and a PhD from TCD (2011). He is co-ordinating a number of Master's courses in nursing, midwifery and cancer care, as well as his teaching role in the college on the BSc in Psychiatric Nursing and MSc Mental Health programmes. He also supervises students from BSc to PhD level.

EARLY INFLUENCES

When Brian was a teenager, he did voluntary work in the community for the benefit of people with intellectual disabilities. This partly influenced his decision to train as a psychiatric nurse. His decision to enter psychiatric nursing as opposed to general nursing was influenced by his gender, as he believed (at the time) general nursing was a female profession. Although his view about this has changed, he believes that the majority of people still hold this view. According to Brian, his family were happy for him to choose whatever he wanted.

After a few years working in the United Kingdom (UK) as a psychiatric nurse, he returned to Dublin in 1995 and worked as a Staff Nurse in St. Patrick's Hospital. He was given many opportunities and strong educational support. He was funded to complete BNS and MSc degrees. Prior to finishing his Bachelor's degree, he was successful in securing a position as Clinical Placement Co-ordinator (CPC), shortly after the introduction of the Diploma in Nursing registration course in 1997. At that time, very few nurses were completing degrees and he completed the BNS in Dublin City University, graduating in 1998. The CPC position was influential, as it carved out an education pathway for him. He was successful in obtaining a post as Acting Nurse Tutor in St. John of God Hospital in 2000. Subsequently, Brian took posts as Nurse Tutor and Clinical Nurse Co-ordinator in St. Patrick's Hospital.

Later in his career, Professor Agnes Higgins and Professor Cecily Begley,[4] who supported him during his PhD study, were very influential leaders for him. The Director of Nursing, Michael Connolly, and the two nurse tutors at St. Patrick's Hospital, Sheelagh Clarke and Tony Cullen, also had a very positive influence. Without those people, he thinks he would not have reached the level of education or self-actualisation he has achieved.

MAJOR LIFE EVENTS

Brian believes that coming back from the UK and working in Dublin was a positive life event. In Ireland, he had opportunities given to him in clinical practice and in progressing into academia as a lecturer. Major life events included those associated with his academic accomplishments. These were all significant and often opened the door to other opportunities. For example, he possibly would not have completed an MSc if he had not had the experience of working in a School of Nursing. This also provided the opportunity to work as a lecturer to Trinity College Dublin (2003) at the introduction of the degree programme. It was while he was there that he decided to pursue a PhD, as he recognised its importance in enhancing his research skills as well as offering him credibility within the third level sector. He co-authored and co-edited a psychiatric/mental health nursing text book that was published by Gill & Macmillan in 2008.

At the beginning of his new career as a nurse lecturer, he was apprehensive about the change as he was unsure of his role and competence in completing research or delivering lectures in a university. The move from clinical practice to academia was a culture shock, as Brian was used to working in a small school with two other tutors and approximately 50 students.

Psychiatric/mental health nursing underpins Brian's teaching and research expertise. He is interested also in the subject of men in nursing. He completed research examining the gender barriers for men in undergraduate general nursing programmes in Ireland. His PhD study explored the experiences of mental health service users

---

[4] **Chapter 5**, *Leadership in Action: Influential Irish Women Nurses' Contribution to Society*, Geraldine McCarthy & Joyce J. Fitzpatrick, Oak Tree Press, 2012.

following discharge from hospital. Using grounded theory, the study found that stigma was a key concern for the participants and this area is now central to his interests and expertise.

CONTRIBUTION TO NURSING

Brian believes that after he completed his PhD, he had a completely different way of thinking about the practice of psychiatric nursing and mental health in Ireland. He wants to share this experience with nursing students so they will be better prepared to care for people with mental health problems. He believes that there needs to be a greater emphasis on psychosocial interventions and that nurses need to be skilled to move away from the medical model. He thinks that communicating with people with mental health problems is critical for mental health service users.

VISION FOR YOUR LIFE'S WORK

As a lecturer, Brian believes that he should be a positive role model for nurses who work with mental health service users. He would like students to value the interpersonal processes that occur between them and the people they care for. He would like to make some changes in the practice of caring for people with mental health problems, where the emphasis should be on the person and not the symptoms. He believes that social exclusion and stigma are major problems for people with mental health problems and they need to be addressed by mental health nurses. He also believes in providing nurses with good communication and interpersonal skills, so that psychiatric nurses can use these more in caring for mental health service users.

COMPETENCIES, STRENGTHS AND VALUES

Brian's values have changed over time. When he was a staff nurse, his values and beliefs were influenced by the medical model of care. When he became an educator and completed his PhD, he started thinking differently about his role. It was only when he was forced to reflect on the practice of psychiatric nursing that he realised the importance of communicating with people with mental health problems and the therapeutic value of this communication. From a competency perspective, Brian has experience of working in the nursing profession for seven years as a staff nurse, three years as a nurse tutor and as a lecturer for the last eight years with many publications to his credit.

CHARACTERISTICS OF LEADERS

Brian believes that a leader has to have a vision; an ability to delegate and motivate others; and the ability to see the strengths and weaknesses of people in order to direct them and to give them the support needed. Communication is a very important characteristic of a good leader, he believes, because those types of leaders are more approachable than others. Good leaders should not be obsessed with power and should be willing to learn from others as well as to share their experiences. They should be reflective; willing to admit their mistakes; visible; and engaged with the work and the people around them. Finally, they should have a sense of humour, a positive relationship with their work, and a positive work/life balance.

SIGNIFICANT CHALLENGES

Brian thinks that he encountered challenges at every point in his career to date. For example, the decision to leave the CPC post and return to a Staff Nurse position was challenging. In addition, making the decision to move to a position as Lecturer in TCD was also challenging. The decision to commence his doctoral work provided further significant challenges.

OPPORTUNITIES THAT ENHANCED SUCCESS

Brian believes that staff from TCD gave him the opportunity to reach his goals; they were very helpful and supportive, especially during his PhD. They gave him some time off to complete his research. He also got financial support from the college and from the Health Research Board.

OBSTACLES ENCOUNTERED AND LESSONS LEARNED

Generally, he thinks that one of his major obstacles is a lack of self-belief. He believes that people with the same character have to challenge themselves to achieve what they want. He learned many lessons from this about challenging yourself, sustaining a belief in yourself and listening to advice from other people. At the end, he says, you have to decide yourself.

ADVICE TO ASPIRING LEADERS

Challenge yourself; have confidence in your abilities; listen to others and look for advice; and recognise when you need to look for help and assistance.

CHAPTER 11
PHILIP LARKIN

Sinéad O'Sullivan

... they radiated energy and a wisdom he found inspirational.

Philip Larkin is Associate Professor of Clinical Nursing (Palliative Care) at the School of Nursing, Midwifery & Health Systems, University College Dublin (UCD) and Our Lady's Hospice, Harold's Cross, Dublin.

Born in Ferns, Co. Wexford, his family "oscillated" between Ireland and the United Kingdom (UK) due to his father's occupation. He was educated mainly in England, attending schools in London and Manchester. He is a Registered General Nurse and a Registered Paediatric Nurse and holds BSc, MSc and PhD degrees. He is Director of the Master's in Palliative Care programme and leads the palliative care research programme within the School of Nursing, Midwifery & Health Systems, UCD.

EARLY INFLUENCES

Philip showed musical talent and from the age of six was boarded at a choral school for musically-gifted children, much to the delight of his father, who was also an aspiring singer. His musical studies gave him a fluency in a number of European languages, and as a result he speaks French and Italian and has a working knowledge of German. His linguistic skills have proved to be of immense benefit to his career. He completed his choral exams and trained as a music teacher. Westminster Cathedral, Downside Abbey and St. Peter's, Wexford were some of the venues where he performed during his musical studies. His career path at this juncture appeared to be as a singer and music teacher.

By 1981, Philip was teaching at the Guildhall School of Music in London, but was not totally happy. He began to think about a change of direction in life. Fortuitously, at that time, there was a 'push' in the London area to get men into nursing, and when a nurse friend told him "this is a great job", his mind was made up. After a particularly "bad day" at the music college, he literally walked out and went to the nearest hospital – Charing Cross – told them he was interested in nursing and would like to apply for entry into their nursing programme. Within 10 days, he was called for interview and immediately was offered a place in the nursing school. Due to the prohibitive cost of living in London, he declined the place at Charing Cross and instead moved to Manchester, which was less expensive and where he had family connections. There he took his general nurse training at the University Hospital of South Manchester.

From the beginning, he liked nursing and found he had a natural affinity for the work. It gave him the job satisfaction he sought. Having qualified, he worked as a staff nurse in orthopaedics and trauma at Addenbrooke's Hospital, Cambridge.

He then decided to study paediatric nursing. He trained and worked in children's nursing, in a hospital grouping that included Great Ormond Street, London and Queen Mary's Hospital, Carshalton, Surrey. On completing this training, he returned to Ireland and worked in Harcourt Street Children's Hospital. As work contracts in Ireland at that time were of very short duration, "literally from week to week", he moved back to Manchester and worked as a Charge Nurse in the bone marrow transplantation unit at the Royal Children's Hospital. While in Manchester, Philip took a BSc degree in Community Nursing (King's College, London), which combined District Nursing and Health Visitation.

While he got a scholarship to study, it was inadequate to cover his living expenses and to supplement his income he worked in paediatrics at the Royal Marsden Hospital, Surrey for the three-year duration of his degree course. Having completed his primary degree, he took up a position as a Health Visitor in a rural district of Oxfordshire, which afforded him the opportunity to do not only the work of Visitor but also some aspects of the work of a District Nurse. During his time at the Royal Marsden and his period as a District Nurse, he became attracted to palliative care, and went on to train in palliative care nursing.

At this point, he had married and he and his wife wished to move back permanently to Ireland. In 1991, the opportunity to do so materialised, when a job as a home care nurse in the Galway Hospice Foundation was advertised. After a period as a Home Care Nurse, he became a Home Care Manager with the Galway Hospice. His arrival in Galway coincided with a time when palliative care was quickly developing in Ireland. As part of that evolution, a movement wishing to cultivate an educational focus grew up and he was seconded to complete a Master's Degree in Health Professional Education (University of Huddersfield). After eight years with the Galway Hospice, Philip took up a post as a Nurse Tutor at Our Lady's Hospice in Harold's Cross, a position he held for three years. He attributes this period to the "take-off" of his palliative care career. As the field of palliative care continued to develop, a post of Regional Manager for the West of Ireland, covering Galway, Mayo and Roscommon, was created. Philip successfully applied for the post, but he remained in the position for only 18 months, as he felt that the job was not fully thought through and the parameters not clearly defined.

Philip has worked with the Irish Sisters of Charity in Harold's Cross since 1998 in various roles and cites this experience as particularly influential. He found they radiated energy and a wisdom that he found inspirational: "There are some incredible women there, such as Sister Francis Rose O'Flynn and Sister Ignatius Phelan, who set up the first Home Care Service in Dublin in response to the needs of the community".

As a result, he impresses upon his students the fact that he can teach them to think critically but they have to develop wisdom themselves. That wisdom is then linked into the judgement that they use clinically and professionally.

Meeting nurses in his role in the European Association of Palliative Care he found really quite enlightening. He saw the challenges that those nurses faced in trying to provide palliative care in circumstances "that one could not even imagine". He has been hugely inspired by their efforts. A colleague and friend in Switzerland, Françoise Pourchez, now retired, who was instrumental in developing palliative care in that region in terms of education, really changed things for people because she wanted to educate. He describes her as an incredible motivator and somebody who really touched him.

MAJOR LIFE EVENTS

There were many challenges and changes during the period that Philip worked in palliative care, coinciding with the introduction of medical consultants. While in Harold's Cross, he ran a Higher Diploma in Palliative Care in conjunction with UCD. When he moved to Galway, he linked up with the National University of Ireland Galway and set up a Higher Diploma programme there, which he ran for a number of years, resulting in him being offered a full-time lectureship.

He then proceeded to complete a PhD at the Catholic University of Louvain. The subject for his doctorate was investigating how people in six European countries, including the UK and Ireland, understood the meaning of dying. His PhD was done using French,

German, Spanish, Italian and English. There were a number of pragmatic reasons for choosing Louvain: (a) "education is heavily subsidised in Belgium", and (b) his linguistic skills were a decided advantage.

Having completed his PhD, Philip was appointed Senior Lecturer at UCD. In 2008, he was appointed Professor of Palliative Care, a joint post between Our Lady's Hospice and UCD.

A request from the incumbent Dr. Tony O'Brien, consultant at Marymount Hospice, Cork to stand for the seat he held on the Board of the European Association of Palliative Care, resulted in Philip serving on the Board for seven years, including a term as Vice President. His time on the Board of the European Association was an enriching experience, offering him a wonderful opportunity to travel, observe and teach all over Europe and beyond.

In 2007, he received the Lifetime Achievement Award from the Macmillan Cancer Support and the *International Journal of Palliative Nursing*, in recognition of his European and international work.

Philip sits on the National Council for Palliative Care in Ireland, with specific responsibility for palliative care education, and is Chair of the Irish Association for Palliative Care. He lectures on palliative and end-of-life care internationally and has published extensively on the subject.

VISION FOR YOUR LIFE'S WORK

Philip believes passionately that palliative care is a human right and should be universally available. He stresses that palliative care has changed and expanded significantly over the years. In the past, the team was called in at the very end. Palliative care now spans chronic illnesses and the team is much more involved throughout the illness trajectory. He describes his vision for palliative and end-of-life care as requiring clear co-operation between the key elements involved to give the people of Ireland the service they deserve. He stresses that palliative care is about people and if we forget that, we lose something very fundamental.

He emphasises the need to involve communities and highlights that compassionate communities must be an integral part of palliative care. Collaboration between the voluntary and the professional bodies, fully supported by the State, is essential. The challenge in Ireland is that there are a lot of players at the table and there is a need to bring them together, citing the motto of the European Association of Palliative Care: "One Voice, One Vision".

COMPETENCIES, STRENGTHS AND VALUES

Philip has always been conscious of a spiritual dimension to his work and, having studied the programme *The Spiritual Art of Living and Dying* over the last four years, he feels that this has allowed him to take stock and he has learned from this the importance of nurturing the very deep thoughts and values that one holds. He cites as an example of this the discipline he developed through his musical training. He now works as a Spiritual Director with other clinicians in the field, not in a religious way, but to help them to tap into their spiritual nature that is part of who they are. How well they express this will impact on the way in which they act, the way in which they respond and the way in which they lead.

Philip has a particular interest in compassion. He sees compassion as the bedrock for palliative care and it must always be present in one's work. He also believes it is a subject that needs further study and exploration, so that we develop compassionate carers and leaders.

One of Philip's strengths is that he is approachable and people feel at ease asking his advice. He has knowledge he shares generously. Within his field, he is looked upon as a visionary person and a transformational leader.

OPPORTUNITIES THAT ENHANCED SUCCESS

Philip feels he has been lucky in that all the choices he has made in his career path were mainly the right decisions. Paediatrics was the right speciality, children's oncology was the right area and he fitted into community nursing with ease. They all linked together and moved him in the direction of palliative care. He feels fortunate to have worked in world-renowned hospitals such as the Royal Marsden. He also cites Our Lady's Hospice, Harold's Cross, Dublin, which is seen internationally as a beacon for hospice and palliative care, and he believes that being able to put these on his *curriculum vitae* helped open doors. He feels fortunate that he has always worked in environments where people supported him and wanted the best for him.

A further career asset was his term on the board of the European Association of Palliative Care, which gave him a huge opportunity to widen his horizons and permitted him to study palliative care in diverse situations, and of course it projected him onto the international stage.

ADVICE TO ASPIRING LEADERS

Don't think too hard about your career, but be flexible; think about it in terms of where you want to go, but allow chance to get in there and let things happen. Remember you might not always make the right decision.

CHAPTER 12
GORDON LYNCH

Lynne Marsh

Never assume that you are actually always right.

Gordon Lynch was born in England of Irish parents. Gordon's parents returned to Waterford and then to Dublin when he was eight years old. Today, Gordon has six children – three girls and three boys – two of whom are adults, and two sets of twins, ages 11 and 13. He now lives in Co. Tipperary with his youngest children and partner.

Gordon completed the three-year Certificate in Psychiatric Nursing in St. Loman's Hospital in Co. Dublin (1981) and then staffed in St. Loman's for six months. Then he went back to the child and adolescent mental health services in Warrenstown House, Dublin and he has specialised in this area for the duration of his nursing career. Gordon completed a MSc in Child & Adolescent Psychoanalytic Psychotherapy through Trinity College Dublin (2000). From this, he developed the first Advanced Nurse Practitioner (ANP) role in mental health in Ireland in Linn Dara Services in Co. Kildare. His other qualifications include management, training, counselling and specialist training in post-traumatic stress disorder (PTSD). The ANP post advanced autonomous practice within the multi-disciplinary team, focusing on the development of a clinical delivery system that met the needs of the service users by reducing waiting lists through solution-focused use of existing resources. His role as ANP required him to work in clinical practice for 50% of the time and he was heavily involved in service development and training for the other half of his post. Gordon recently retired from the Health Service Executive (HSE) but remains active in nursing and psychotherapy. He is the nursing representative on the Child & Adolescent Mental Health Services (CAMHS) Advisory Group to the Department of Health.

EARLY INFLUENCES

For the first year or two when Gordon was working in Warrenstown House, he had no predefined plans and had not intended to stay there. An influential figure for Gordon was Professor William Yule, the Co-ordinator of Warrenstown House's activities. One of Professor Yule's main areas of interest was in post-traumatic stress disorders (PTSD) in young people, which ignited Gordon's interest in the topic. Gordon was very keen to continue professional development but there was no funding at the time for any graduate courses which for nurses were only beginning to emerge. However, he went on a two-day course to the newly-renovated Royal Hospital, Donnybrook and there he listened to an American woman, Vera Fahlberg, who at the time was a renowned expert in child protection. She had a significant impact on Gordon and influenced his thinking considerably. She spoke for two days without notes. Most of her talks dealt with exposure to people outside of where you work and train. She supported the notion that it was not good to be insular within your profession but to look outside of where you are and to grasp opportunities that encourage you to change practice positively. Inevitably, Gordon is of the firm belief that it is healthier for the profession to look outside of nursing and to be open-minded. To one degree or another, mental health problems are associated with life's difficulties and therefore it is imperative that we look outside the box.

MAJOR LIFE EVENTS

Gordon's time in Warrenstown House was completely accidental but, once there, if he were to cite an individual in nursing that influenced him it would be Peadar McCabe, Assistant Chief Nursing Officer, Child Psychiatric Services, who also retired last year. Mr McCabe was the Assistant Director of Nursing of Warrenstown House when Gordon started working there and was a very positive influence for Gordon.

CONTRIBUTION TO NURSING

Gordon's contribution to nursing has spanned 30 years. He is a very humble man and really believes that he did not make any one significant change overall. However, Gordon held the first ANP post in mental health services in Ireland. He attributes the success of this post to the abundance of support that he received from the National Council for the Professional Development of Nursing & Midwifery and from Mary Farrelly in particular. The ANP post facilitated Gordon to develop a system that looked at waiting lists and how staff were able to manage individual clinical loads. With support from staff, Gordon developed systems in South Kildare that they called at the time 'therapeutic initial assessment'. Prior to the implementation of this assessment, children and adolescents with mental health issues and their families were maintained on long waiting lists. This was an unsatisfactory process and, prior to meeting the individuals, sources of information came from a number of people, such as General Practitioners (GPs) and referral agents. Once the referral was reviewed by Gordon, decisions were made in relation to scheduling a meeting or referring the person to an appropriate service if necessary. People became frustrated with lengthy waiting lists; according to research in Ireland, the United Kingdom and the United States, the most important single thing to service users is how soon they can be seen. Consequently, once an appropriate referral is made, it is mandated now that a first meeting takes place as quickly as possible to identify the best way forward. Gordon was the first point of contact and scheduled the first meeting with the client and their family and ensured a solution-focused approach. Gordon ensured that a first meeting never ended because of time constraints, which was a very positive approach and gave the clear message that individuals would be listened to and heard. Most of the meetings ended after an hour and a half or two hours but it also meant that all of the administration work attached to the case was completed and follow-up referrals made where necessary. Gordon was receiving in excess of 250 referrals a year and subsequently met with about 90 of the referrals. Over the four years, over half (52%) did not require a second appointment and positive responses from service users, referral agents and especially GPs were noted.

Gordon is an author of the chapter on Childhood & Adolescent Mental Health Problems in *Psychiatric/Mental Health Nursing* (Morrissey, Keogh & Doyle, 2008) and other articles. Gordon was chair of the Irish Branch of ACAMH (Association for Child and Adolescent Mental Health) and was the nursing representative on the CAMHS committee in *Vision for Change*. Additionally, he was the only nurse or Irish person to sit on the Council of ACAMH in London and was the founder chair of FINCAMH (Forum in Ireland for Nurses in Child & Adolescent Mental Health).

VISION FOR YOUR LIFE'S WORK

Gordon does not seek the limelight and just feels that, whatever you do, you must do your job right. If you are doing it properly and if you do what you are supposed to be doing, then you are fulfilling your life's work.

COMPETENCIES, STRENGTHS, AND VALUES

According to Gordon, you need to be continuously training and to be enthusiastic about any opportunities for continuing personal and professional development. Gordon believes that people should take opportunities available, as competencies and strengths come from the things you learn. He believes that nurse training prepares you for life both professionally and personally. Gordon's experience as an employee with the HSE has been entirely positive both on a corporate level and within his own service.

CHARACTERISTICS OF LEADERS

People who are visible to others are good leaders. Leaders should be prepared to question the conventional wisdom and to recognise that there are different ways of doing things that do not necessarily conflict but may be quite different.

SIGNIFICANT CHALLENGES

When Gordon became Assistant Chief Nursing Officer, he found it significantly challenging as he realised that his niche was in clinical work and managing clinical systems and not in managing people.

OPPORTUNITIES THAT ENHANCED SUCCESS

If he had remained as a Staff Nurse, Gordon would have been perfectly happy. However, following the Commission of Nursing and the development of the ANP pathway, a defining moment in his career was presented and the new post allowed him to maintain his clinical competence and engage in frontline nursing. It facilitated a promotional pathway that was traditionally only seen in management and the remuneration also acknowledged the clinical competence and educational requirements befitting of such a post.

OBSTACLES ENCOUNTERED AND LESSONS LEARNED

Fortunately, obstacles experienced by Gordon over his career were few. On the very practical day-to-day basis working in a specialised area was a help, because that was where opportunities lay as child and adolescent mental health services were developing in Ireland

ADVICE TO ASPIRING LEADERS

Gordon thinks that those who pursue leadership for the sake of it are probably not leaders. You need to see things done well and thoroughly without fear of upset. You need to get on very well with staff but if you have a problem, deal with it. Avail of every opportunity to learn how things are done elsewhere. Never assume that you are actually always right.

CHAPTER 13
PETER McLOONE

Nicola Cornally

*Start with enthusiasm. You must have enthusiasm, belief in
yourself and be able to communicate and share that
enthusiasm with others.*

Peter McLoone qualified as a psychiatric nurse in 1972 and
practiced in St. Luke's Hospital in Clonmel for almost 10 years.
Simultaneously, he worked at local level to build up a branch of the
Psychiatric Nurses Association (PNA). In 1979, he took a full-time
post as a trade union official. He went on to serve as General

Secretary of the Irish Municipal, Public & Civil Trade Union (IMPACT) from 1995 to his retirement in 2010. He was a member of the Executive of the Irish Congress of Trade Unions (ICTU) for 17 years, was elected Vice President in 2003 and served as President of ICTU from 2005 to 2007. He was a Board member of An Bord Altranais and Beaumont Hospital for almost 11 years. Peter also served as Chairman of FÁS (the Irish Training and Employment Authority) from 2006 to 2007. Currently, he is a board member of the Labour Relations Commission and is on the governing body of the National College of Ireland and the Playing for Life charity. Most recently, he was appointed to The Irish Times Trust.

EARLY INFLUENCES

Peter was born in Ballyshannon, Co. Donegal. His father, Bill, was a tradesman and there were five in the family: four boys and a girl. They were raised in Donegal and they all went on to have a career in the public service. Peter describes his family, in particular his mother, as having an influence in terms of his achievements in education. She continually emphasised the importance of completing secondary level education. He admits that, growing up in the 1960s, university was out of reach, but the encouragement was to do something successfully and have a career, and this is what each of his siblings did. A good education was seen as the foundation of a good future. While his mother and father were influential early on, Peter feels that most of the influence came later on in his nursing career. His teachers and family members influenced his values and character more so than the choices he made in his career.

In terms of his nursing career, the people who influenced him included John Corbett and Andy Hickey. He worked with them, building up the branch of the PNA at a local level. His nurse tutors, Therese Hickey and Nora Doherty, also were influential in many ways and he reflects on how they had the ability to relate theory to actual life, which made exam preparation and practice seamless.

He was a member of An Board Altranais for eight years, where he worked with and met inspiring individuals. As he got into the representative role, he was inspired by the first Nursing Advisor to the Department of Health and Children (Peta Taaffe[5]). Within this role, she was considered a token representative, but he remembers that there was nothing token about her. She realised that huge investment was needed to move nursing from diploma to graduate and then to the university and he admired her visionary qualities.

He worked closely with Liam Doran (see **Chapter 6**), General Secretary of the Irish Nurses & Midwives Organisation, and has great regard for him, describing him as the best advocate and representative for the nursing profession. He recalls Liam's capacity to represent even the most qualified of specialists and his ability to demonstrate that, to do a job effectively, you needed to be able to understand what people did, what their role was and articulate that effectively. He describes Liam as a true leader and his style of leadership influenced Peter in his representative role.

MAJOR LIFE EVENTS

Two key events shaped his thinking and values early on in life.

The first occurred when Peter had just finished second level education. His mother had a disorder of the pituitary gland and was in hospital for almost a year. Peter stayed at home during this period to run the household and his contact with the hospital and home services, as a family member, demonstrated to him the importance of a well-structured public service. Following this period in his life, he started applying for jobs and one of them was a trainee psychiatric nurse position in St. Luke's Hospital in Clonmel. Peter intended just completing his training there but ended up staying for almost 10 years.

A second key event in his life was the death of his brother in the late 1970s, who as a result of melanoma required substantial dealings with the health services. Not only was this a challenging time in Peter's life, from a personal perspective, it also confirmed for him the desire to be part of a union that worked for a better public sector. This major life event coincided with the beginning of his career as a full-time trade union official. The importance of a quality public service is something that he came to realise when his

---

[5]   **Chapter 21**, *Leadership in Action: Influential Irish Women Nurses' Contribution to Society*, Geraldine McCarthy & Joyce J. Fitzpatrick, Oak Tree Press, 2012.

brother was brought home from hospital to be nursed. He firmly believes that the quality of public services mark the quality of our society and it not only defines us but gives us our humanity. This conviction stuck with him over the lifetime of his career.

VISION FOR YOUR LIFE'S WORK

Peter claims that his career naturally evolved from his initial role as a representative locally in St. Luke's (which began when he was a final year student nurse). He believed that student nurses were not getting a fair deal and there were a number of issues that drove him to recognise that you can complain or become involved and seek to do something about an issue. This philosophy held when he qualified as a nurse, and he stayed active in the local branch of the PNA with John Corbett and Andy Hickey. Following, this he took up a role at national level and became National Secretary. He was invited by Phil Flynn, then General Secretary of the Irish Congress of Trade Unions (ICTU), to work full-time with ICTU to develop and increase its membership both in nursing and other health professions. His career thus evolved into other areas of union membership, other than nursing and health professions. He applied for and became National Secretary for the union and then General Secretary.

Peter is unsure that his career was as a result of a vision but he was always preoccupied with the future and believed that, by taking up positions, you can make things better. Being a member of the Nursing Board and Beaumont Hospital for 11 years opened doors for Peter and he emphasises the importance of exposing oneself to opportunities, in addition to what you do for a living. These all contribute to what equips you to move from one level, from one role, into the next. He states that it is not something you can study and just decide you are ready to do a certain job; there is a lot of prior experience and exposure needed first.

COMPETENCIES, STRENGTHS AND VALUES

As a result of his representative roles, Peter understands the importance of being capable of taking initiative, to have resolve and possess an understanding that, to be successful, you have to be more preoccupied with the future than the past and have a deep sense of self. Peter acknowledges that he was never satisfied with the *status quo* and, without being egotistical about it, developed a sense of optimism that he could make things better. This drive was underpinned by the values that his parents instilled, primarily to always have integrity. Peter believes that, as time goes on, you add to that armoury. He recalls Phil Flynn saying "the day you stop learning is the day you stop adding value". Similarly, his father believed that knowledge, unlike any other commodity, increased with use. Accordingly, Peter recognises knowledge as a key competency of good leadership. In addition, Peter emphasises the importance of having a high level of personal ambition and motivation, and the ability to listen to people and learn from conversations. He firmly acknowledges, particularly when discharging a role such as General Secretary of IMPACT, that you must have the ability to motivate, not just individuals, but also groups and be able to set and define realistic attainable goals. From his extensive career in the public sector, he is certain that you will not get far without patience and understanding, which are fundamental to good communication. He describes other key competencies as being objective and having the ability to take and give constructive criticism. He states that you need to be the type of character that can make and take tough decisions and be fair. Finally, Peter recommends a healthy sense of humour.

CHARACTERISTICS OF LEADERS

Peter recognises a good leader as somebody who attracts and selects the right people. He explains that, as a leader, you are looking for people who have a clear expectation of what is required, what is expected, and what is needed to deliver. Peter feels that a good leader always will praise and recognise the contributions of others and always care for people. He argues that, in society, the strongest allies of the public services must be the people it serves and central to all campaigns is better services, fairer deals and better quality of life for everybody. From a union perspective, he believes that there should be an emphasis on 'we are here to serve the public', not simply to serve the interests of the people who are in membership. In his opinion, the two go hand-in-hand and, if you are not genuinely committed, then the general public will not be allies of the causes that you advocate, because their cause should be your cause.

SIGNIFICANT CHALLENGES

Peter admits there were a lot of challenges along the way, but no negative memories. He recalls being Chairman of FÁS (2006 to 2007) as the most significant challenge he faced. Micheál Martin (the Minister for Enterprise, Trade & Employment at the time) asked him to take up the position, which he did readily. However, it was fraught with controversy, which he had neither anticipated nor desired. The challenge was amplified owing to his co-existing role as General Secretary of IMPACT. He recounts that all of the bad press about FÁS began with the headline "Peter McLoone, General Secretary of IMPACT ...", which meant that the union and its members were getting negative press when they had no involvement or affiliation with FÁS. This created a lot of stress in Peter's life. But the characteristics he developed over the years, such as resilience and resolve, allowed him to work through the issues and emerge from the situation unscathed.

OPPORTUNITIES THAT ENHANCED SUCCESS

As a final year student nurse, Peter took the decision to represent student nurses at a local level. This opportunity presented itself and he had the aptitude to appreciate that things could not change simply because you were griping about them or you were demanding change; change had to be something that you worked for and influenced. When he went to the union representatives with the students' issues, they concurred that things needed to change and in a way challenged him to act in a representative role. Peter seized the opportunity and this, together with hard work and external involvement on various boards, lead him to the eventual role of General Secretary of IMPACT.

Peter contends that people need to work together, believing that if you engage with issues in a collective way, with a single purpose, there is a chance that you will make a difference. Over his career, he came to recognise that achievements do not happen by chance, you do not get lucky breaks and everything that you achieve has to be planned for, worked for and at times even struggled for. He believes that, if you do not work with a good team, you will experience more failures than success.

OBSTACLES ENCOUNTERED AND LESSONS LEARNED

In his role as General Secretary of IMPACT, obstacles were inevitable and each campaign brought about its own set of issues. However, he believes that you go through experiences and reflect, you question why things went wrong, why it did not work out as planned. On reflection, he feels that certain things did not work out because the message of the trade unions still remains very poorly understood. What has been achieved tends to be underappreciated. But the lesson he learned from each campaign was to act collectively, to work together, and to create a vision that demonstrates the collective strength. Peter remembers the period before the benchmarking exercise (salaries for comparable grades were agreed by the government) and states that the public service was characterised by a litany of different disputes and threats. It seemed to the public that union members were living in a world that was completely detached from them. The 1980s, and even more so the 1990s, were very difficult times for Peter, and he recounts that at the time the union lost control. However, he believes that the work conducted in the 2000s led to the creation of benchmarking, which brought stability, and a great sense of purpose. He is confident that it would not have been possible to put the Croke Park Agreement (cuts in services agreed with trade unions) together were it not for the work of the preceding 10 years, which dealt with the experiences of the late 1990s. In essence, each obstacle provided learning and this became the foundation for future decision-making. Peter reiterates the importance of collectivism, stating that it gives authority, not individual existence and individual sense of importance over another.

ADVICE TO ASPIRING LEADERS

You must have enthusiasm, belief in yourself and be able to communicate and share that enthusiasm with others. You are going to be required to manage what other people say, to develop other people and to lead. So you must take the four qualities – manage, motivate, develop, lead – and remember it is always important that these skills are underpinned by an enthusiasm that will allow other people to acknowledge and accept you in a leadership role. It is important that you have good people around you who have a clear understanding of your expectations. Never understate the importance of caring for the people who work with you and for you and always be fulsome in your praise and recognition for the contribution that they are making. Do not think you can achieve anything without support. Avoid doing things on the basis that you are going to get something back, as you will be sorely disappointed. Be engaging and recognise the contribution and the attributes of others.

CHAPTER 14
BRENDAN NOONAN

Saed Azizeh

*Leaders must be close enough to relate to others but far
enough ahead to motivate them.*

Brendan Noonan was born, raised, and educated in Fermoy, Co.
Cork, where he lives with his wife, Sinead, and their two children,
Roisin and Ciara. He is the youngest of three, and has one brother
and one sister. Being the youngest meant that, while he was not
disadvantaged in any way and never wanted for anything, he did
feel that he had to work a little harder to be heard and to prove that

he could do just as well if not better than his siblings, in all the usual growing-up activities, from hurling to racquetball. Since his childhood, Brendan was termed by his family and friends as 'ultra-competitive', or having a 'must-win attitude'. His parents often remind him how badly he took defeat, from walkouts to going on strike. While he hopes that his own children would take defeat honourably, he thinks that this early competitive nature has stood him well in his career development. Brendan holds a Diploma in Nursing (National University of Ireland Galway, 1998); a BSc (University College Cork, 2001); a Higher Diploma in Ear, Nose & Throat Nursing (Royal College of Surgeons in Ireland, 2003); a MSc (University College Cork (UCC), 2006); a Postgraduate Diploma in Teaching & Learning (UCC, 2010) and is currently a Doctoral student at UCC. He works as a Lecturer/Practitioner at the School of Nursing & Midwifery, UCC.

EARLY INFLUENCES

Brendan's parents played a major role in influencing who he is and what he stands for. His father was – and still is – a hardworking man, with a strong work ethic. His mother is a practicing nurse. He always was captivated by the stories that his mother told him about her work day, the people she met and cared for, the difficulties she encountered in everyday people's lives and the simple things that could be done to alleviate some of the suffering. His parents were able to offer him a good quality of life. His mother always seemed to have a good work/life balance and genuinely appeared to be very content in her work – thus, the seedlings of interest in nursing were firmly planted. Being the only male nurse in the group during Brendan's training as a student nurse in Limerick Regional Hospital (1995 to 1998) was a unique experience. While initially overwhelmed by this situation, the support and friendship that he received from his fellow students and friends outside of nursing was incredible. He also learnt that gender in nursing is irrelevant; the entire group was professional and well-educated. In Brendan's opinion, gender does not matter; it is all about how well you provide care.

Brendan has worked with nurses and physicians who have been true role models, critical decision-makers and educators, providing remarkable care. This has made him develop his career to be a person who has knowledge to impart to people, to share with and inspire them.

A year or so after completing his training in Limerick, he moved to Cork and began working as a Staff Nurse in a surgical ward of the South Infirmary Victoria University Hospital (SIVUH). On the first day, he met with his Clinical Nurse Manager, who has been the most inspiring person in his career to date. She was highly motivated, immensely energetic, and displayed a real interest in her team, from the nurses on the unit to the people in the kitchen, so as to ensure that patients who journeyed through the unit would experience only the best possible quality of care. He remembered quite clearly that she used to keep a file on every nurse who worked on the unit, a file that was compiled privately between both parties, discussing areas such as career goals, special interests and agreeing on the steps required to achieve these goals. She ensured that every individual nurse was accountable for a specific area of practice development, so that they could all begin creating their very own career portfolios. In that particular unit, patient and family care and contributions to the unit as a whole were always acknowledged and celebrated, even in difficult and busy times. Staff worked hard on the unit; they wanted to do their very best, and they were inspired by their leader. In addition, this manager was willing also to make changes that were not always welcomed but were necessary. She was a strong believer who stood alongside staff in difficult times, a great listener, an advocate, a person who you would have no hesitation in approaching for advice and a friendly ear.

Brendan describes himself as being lucky in meeting people who have a positive outlook and who provide him with a sense of positivity.

MAJOR LIFE EVENTS

Brendan met some genuinely inspiring teachers who instilled within him a sense of community and giving. Perhaps the final influencing factor was when he travelled to Lourdes with the Cloyne Dioceses two years prior to his Leaving Certificate. The trip was organised by a voluntary movement, bringing the sick, disabled and underprivileged to the Marian shrine. Brendan joined a large community of priests, lay people, helpers and students. He travelled and worked with them for a week. He knew after spending one of the best weeks of his life that a career where he could continue to work closely with people, communicating with people, caring for their needs so as to enhance their quality of life and sense of hope was the career for him. Lourdes was such a positive experience, generating a warm feeling inside that he could make someone feel better, happier and more content, even with the limited skills that he had prior to his formal training. Another major life event was being in the second group of student nurses who did the three-year diploma in the University of Limerick.

CONTRIBUTION TO NURSING

Brendan has a saying over his desk at work that states, "We are what we repeatedly do; excellence is not an act but a habit". He tries to do the simple things well; he tries to do the right things all of the time. Throughout his years as a nurse, working with fellow colleagues and particularly in his role as a Lecturer/Practitioner in the School of Nursing, he hopes that his actions both in clinical and in education have inspired people to learn more, to do more, to become more and to dream more. He remembers a Professor in the School telling him one day that we all need to have a vision. It is not about making major changes to become a leader, but he firmly believes that a leader is someone who inspires people to become more and to dream more, to have a vision. He considers that this has been his greatest contribution to nursing to date, that he has hopefully become an aspirational role model.

At present, Brendan is working as a Lecturer/Practitioner in UCC, where he has been since 2005. This is an innovative role developed by Professor Geraldine McCarthy,[6] Professor and Head/Dean of School of Nursing & Midwifery at the time. As part of his role, Brendan spends half his time in clinical practice with students in the South Infirmary, Victoria University Hospital, Cork. He spends the remaining time in the School of Nursing in UCC, teaching the undergraduate and postgraduate programmes. Brendan takes the role of supernumerary staff alongside students who are in clinical placement and in an assigned unit; they take a caseload for the whole shift in an attempt to translate the theoretical side of learning and to apply it in the clinical arena. He hopes that, in his role as Lecturer/Practitioner, he can narrow the theory/practice gap both for the students and the staff nurses on the unit.

Since qualifying as a nurse, he has continued with his professional development, right up to where he is now, which is close to finishing his doctorate.

VISION FOR YOUR LIFE'S WORK

Brendan wants to continue in his role as Lecturer/Practitioner, whilst also continuing to conduct research surrounding cancer care. Working as a Lecturer/Practitioner is difficult to manage at times. However, Brendan feels that this gives him time in the college to teach, which he loves. In addition, this role allows him to spend time with students in clinical practice and keep himself up-to-date with developments, which, in turn, increases his credibility as a teacher. Additionally, it equips him with many real clinical examples for use in the classroom. Being able to tell students a story from real practice and relate it to theory in the classroom means so much to students.

Brendan wants to continue to work on building a national and international reputation for scholarship and outstanding research in clinical nursing and practice development. His doctoral research focused on exploring the experiences of oral cancer patients over their cancer trajectory, findings from which potentially will inform

---

[6] **Chapter 15**, *Leadership in Action: Influential Irish Women Nurses' Contribution to Society*, Geraldine McCarthy & Joyce J. Fitzpatrick, Oak Tree Press, 2012.

an intervention to improve and enhance the quality of the experience for oral cancer patients.

In the future, he would love to hold a position as joint Professor in Clinical Nursing, a role that has been recently piloted between School of Nursing, Midwifery & Health Systems at University College Dublin (UCD), the Mater Hospital and St. Vincent's Hospital, Dublin. These are truly exciting and innovative new positions, aimed at providing a nursing-specific contribution to both research strategy and nursing practice development. At present, he is completing the steps necessary to apply for such a position.

COMPETENCIES, STRENGTHS AND VALUES

From a competency perspective, Brendan has experience of working in the nursing profession for the last 14 years and in the academic arena for the last six years. One of his greatest strengths is commitment. He has always demonstrated great commitment to both his professional duties and his professional development. He considers himself responsible and loyal.

In addition to his Lecturer/Practitioner role, he has many other diverse roles: for example, he also co-ordinates undergraduate student placement and experience in SIVUH, a role requiring management, organisational, and interpersonal skills and is a member of the National Executive Committee of the Irish Association for Nurses in Oncology (IANO), an organisation committed to promoting a sense of community amongst cancer nurses across Ireland.

Brendan's personal value system is based on solid, rational reasoning, and responsible decision-making. He values people who have integrity (are trustworthy and honest); in other words, you know what to expect from them. He knows that they will act honourably and do what they believe to be right. He also values respect, treating people with fairness and courtesy. According to Brendan, people who accept responsibility are dependable and willing to be accountable for their actions.

CHARACTERISTICS OF LEADERS

Leaders have to be visionary and dream of how they want their practice, unit, or college to develop. In addition, a leader should be an educator, innovator, motivator, communicator, advisor and facilitator. Leaders have to be dynamic.

SIGNIFICANT CHALLENGES

From a national and global perspective, health care reform is always on the agenda. Brendan thinks that nurses will need to prepare themselves to deal with complex comprehensive patient care in the home. Nursing roles will continue to expand, new positions will be created, home care will embrace tele-health, and lifestyle change will be paramount. Nurse practitioners will see greater demand for them to become frontline providers. Brendan thinks that the demand for nursing expertise will rise astronomically over the coming years, providing opportunity for nurses but a significant challenge for nurse educators. Another challenge is the need for greater involvement of nurse leaders, educators and clinicians in shaping the future of health care, and providing a unified voice for nursing.

OPPORTUNITIES THAT ENHANCED SUCCESS

One of the best opportunities he had was during his nurse training, when he met his best friend who later became his wife, Sinead, a woman with patience and a kind and supporting soul that anyone would wish to spend their lives with.

Another opportunity that had an influence on Brendan's life was the experience of being in the second group of students in Ireland to undertake a national newly established, State-funded, three-year Diploma in Nursing Studies affiliated with the University of Limerick. This afforded him the opportunity to complete a BSc degree in nursing in one year (in University College Cork in 2001) and thus began his academic development.

OBSTACLES ENCOUNTERED AND LESSONS LEARNED

Brendan has found time management a challenge. He has improved over the years by giving himself and asking people for time deadlines. Another challenge is that of working to live *versus* living to work. Brendan looks forward to challenges and views them not as roadblocks, but as opportunities.

ADVICE TO ASPIRING LEADERS

Brendan believes that people grow from experience and become stronger. He draws immense strength and support from his wife and family, friends, and close colleagues. He remembers a truly inspirational community leader telling him early on in his career to surround himself with positive people, a team that will be bubbling over to help each other; he has been trying to do this in his life.

Each person defines himself by his own actions. A leader's performance is measured by the people who follow and how they inspire and engage. Taking time out on your own is important. This opens the mind, gives you time to reflect and problem solve. He has often found solutions to different situations while out jogging, or mountain-biking, through 'eureka' moments.

CHAPTER 15

BARRY O'BRIEN

Mary Rose Day

Paralysis through analysis.

Barry O'Brien is the National Director of Human Resources in the Health Service Executive (HSE), the largest employer in the State, with more than 67,000 direct employees, and a further 35,000 employed by agencies funded by it. Human Resources (HR) is responsible for developing and supporting an organisational structure and culture that is client/patient-focused and empowers staff to realise their potential in a safe and healthy working environment. Its role is diverse and involves managing staff turnover, recruitment, ensuring skill mix, staff training and maintenance of industrial relations.

After qualifying and while working as a staff nurse, Barry pursued further studies at University College Cork, which included a Diploma in Social Studies and a Diploma in Pharmacology. He worked as a Staff Nurse, mostly in Cork University Hospital (CUH) and was appointed Assistant Director of Nursing in South Lee Mental Health Services in 1992, and Employee Relations Manager (Southern Health Board) in 1998. He completed a Higher Diploma in Personnel Management, and is currently a Fellow of the Chartered Institute of Personnel & Development (CIPD). In 2005, he became the Employee Relations Manager, and later the National Director for Human Resources, for HSE South. In March 2008, he moved to Dublin and became the National Director for Human Resources and worked with the National Hospitals Office as the Head of HR and was the Lead Executive for the Implementation of the Consultant Contract in 2008.

EARLY INFLUENCES

Barry's father came from Barryroe in West Cork and his mother from Innishannon and both worked in Barryroe Co-op. He was the middle child and has two brothers and two sisters. He was educated at St. Fachtna's de La Salle, Skibbereen and completed his mental health nursing qualification in Our Lady's Hospital, Lee Road, Cork in 1979. Barry's father and mother played a very influential role in his life and instilled in him a sense of community and fairness.

He was highly influenced also by the legendary General Practitioner, Dr. Micheál O'Sullivan and by Diarmuid O'Donovan, Principal of the National School in Skibbereen. Both of these people were very committed to their communities and were very engaged with young people, the Gaelic Athletic Association and community development. They were very influential in grounding his beliefs.

In his earlier years, Barry represented young people in Skibbereen, was a member of the Community Council for a number of years and was Chairman of the Youth Club. Barry describes himself as being a 'people's person', who is very interested in society and equity.

Michael Cottrell, Director of Mental Health Nursing, played a key role in his career advancement. He was hugely supportive, saw people's potential, gave people opportunities to advance ideas and, under his guidance, ideas were realised. This helped Barry advance from being a Staff Nurse directly to being the Assistant Director of Nursing, which would have been unusual at that time. Sean Hurley, former Chief Executive Officer of the Southern Health Board, was a man way before his time in his thinking and his management style. He was widely respected and was able to get extra from a number of staff and he also influenced Barry.

A further influence was the CUH campus. The environment there was an exceptional place for learning from the point of view of developing management and leadership skill sets. Services Managers meetings took place every Tuesday morning in the Board Room. People from diverse disciplines such as nursing, therapies and laboratory staff attended these meetings. Some of these people were exceptional and they contributed hugely to the overall way in which CUH ran its services. Barry represented Mental Health Services at these meetings and this environment was a key influence in his personal development.

MAJOR LIFE EVENTS

A major life event for Barry was getting married. His wife, Mary, has been an influence and his number one supporter and he would not be where he is today without her support. Mary and his two daughters (Karen and Gillian) are a huge part of his life.

From a personal perspective and from a manager's perspective, one of his best achievements was the opening of the €75 million Cork Unified Maternity Hospital. The bringing together of three hospitals into a new work environment has turned out to be a fantastic success.

CONTRIBUTION TO NURSING

Barry's major contribution to nursing has been his commitment to promoting and supporting change within the mental health services. As a result, there have been advances in the area of mental health and dedicated funding and budgets are now provided for the development of mental health services. Barry has worked hard to change the dynamics of mental health nursing and the model of care has moved from an institutional model to a patient/person-centred model.

VISION FOR YOUR LIFE'S WORK

Barry's vision for his life work is his strong sense of purpose. He is quite passionate about what he does and he believes in doing the best that he can within the resources available. These are very difficult times but there are some superb people working in the health services. His vision is to maximise his own potential and give his best and at the same time, to maximise the potential of the people that he works with so that they too give their best.

COMPETENCIES, STRENGTHS AND VALUES

Barry does not shirk making decisions. He has a very good knowledge of the health service after working for 36 years in diverse roles and areas and in strategic positions. These experiences and the people he has met and worked with inform his thinking. He is a straight talker and he likes to say things as he sees them and sometimes that may be too quickly. His key strengths are as a team player, he is fair and loyal to people. Over the years, it has never been about the grade the person is at; it always has been about the contribution the person can make. Barry values people, their loyalty, hard work, and commitment to doing the best that they can in all instances.

CHARACTERISTICS OF LEADERS

Barry believes that leaders are visible, honest and trustworthy; have the ability to listen; give clarity of thought in their purpose; and are decision-makers with a focus on achieving and implementing to the greatest extent possible. Barry firmly believes that it is very important for leaders to maximise what everyone agrees on and implement it. He believes at times that nursing leadership does not represent what nurses are thinking. Barry believes that having a voice and not being afraid to offer views and opinions are very important. Leaders need to be aware that the best ideas in many instances come from where they are least expected. Leaders need to create an open environment that gives everybody the opportunity to make a contribution.

SIGNIFICANT CHALLENGES

Health is a very big business and it has many stakeholders and the Irish public values health. Significant challenges are resources and matching people's expectations with reality. Improving management capacity and implementing best practice processes in a time of scarce resources are significant challenges.

OPPORTUNITIES THAT ENHANCED SUCCESS

The opportunities that enhance success are accepting that change is a constant. Barry could never have envisaged that he would become National Head of HR for the HSE after 36 years of service. Trust and credibility in being able to deliver were placed in him and thus enhanced his opportunities.

OBSTACLES ENCOUNTERED AND LESSONS LEARNED

Obstacles encountered have been "paralysis through analysis" and the lack of accountability for personal performance and delivery of services.

ADVICE TO ASPIRING LEADERS

Barry's advice is to be true to yourself and not to expect anything to happen overnight as things happen at the most unexpected times. Keep your mind open to new ideas and value everybody you meet in your work environment.

Barry's nursing background has given him exceptional experience and insight into the challenges faced by frontline staff. Barry has met some incredibly dedicated and committed people, who have made a difference to the lives of those who have used the services.

CHAPTER 16
DAMIEN O'DOWD

Teresa Wills

Hard work and commitment pays off.

Damien O'Dowd is Chief Executive of Bloomfield Health Services, located in Rathfarnham, Dublin. The service was established by the Quakers in Ireland in 1812 and was based in Donnybrook, Dublin until 2005, when it moved to its current location in a state-of-the-art purpose-built facility. Bloomfield Health Services is a provider of specialist services to older persons in mental health, dementia specific and medical services. The facility has two main services:

Bloomfield Hospital (a teaching hospital of Trinity College Dublin), which is registered with the Mental Health Commission as an approved centre, and New Lodge Nursing Home, which is registered with the Health Information & Quality Authority. Damien completed his psychiatric nurse training in St. John of God Hospital, Stilorgan, Dublin, qualifying as a Registered Psychiatric Nurse in 1988. He completed an 18-month postgraduate general nursing programme in St. Michael's Hospital, Dun Laoghaire (qualifying as a general nurse in 1990); a Diploma in Counselling at the National University of Ireland Maynooth (1991); a Diploma in Nursing Management at the Royal College of Surgeons in Ireland (RCSI) (1992); a BA in Management in the Institute of Public Administration (2001); and a MBA in Health Services Management at the Michael Smurfit Graduate School of Business at University College Dublin (2006). Currently, he is undertaking his Doctorate in Governance at Queen's University Belfast.

Damien worked as a Staff Nurse in Psychiatric Nursing at St. John of God Hospital, Dublin and in General Nursing at St. Vincent's University Hospital, Elm Park, Dublin. He returned to St. John of God Hospital, and progressed from Staff Nurse to Clinical Nurse Manager to Director of Nursing within his first 10 years there. In 2007, he was appointed as Head of Operations & Quality at St. John of God Hospital. Four years later, he was appointed to his current position of Chief Executive at Bloomfield Health Services. Damien is also a guest lecturer with the RCSI and an independent surveyor with Comparative Health Knowledge System (CHKS) in the United Kingdom, which is a leading provider of business intelligence, and performance improvement services in the health care sector.

EARLY INFLUENCES

Damien is the eldest of four children and grew up in Bray, Co. Dublin. His parents played an influential role. They had a strong work ethic and were very encouraging in relation to studying and working hard. This has stayed with him, and he always regarded this as an integral part of life as opposed to an additional task. Damien recalls a career guidance teacher, who saw qualities in him and advised him to consider a career that would allow him to work with people.

MAJOR LIFE EVENTS

The opportunity to study in psychiatric nursing in 1985 marked the beginning of his working life, yet he had never intended nursing as a career. He had considered pursuing a career in science and was offered a place in science just after the offer for nursing which he had accepted. Entering psychiatric nursing was his first experience of health care and was a major life event. He subsequently undertook general nurse training, but particularly enjoyed psychiatry, hence he kept coming back to it. He got experience elsewhere as a general staff nurse; however, psychiatry was his focus and he is still associated with that area of work today.

CONTRIBUTION TO NURSING

One of his projects in the early 1990s was the introduction of Primary Nursing. He was a member of a team that successfully introduced the Primary Nursing concept, which was a precursor to the clinical team key worker in use today. This was a significant advancement in the early 1990s for delivery of mental health nursing care. Damien subsequently became involved in the Quality in Action concept and in mental health care in Ireland. This area of interest has remained with Damien, both in his position as Head of Operations & Quality and as a surveyor for CHKS. Indeed, as a chief executive, quality is one of his key underlying principles.

Professional development has always been a key area of interest for Damien. In his role as Director of Nursing, he made a significant contribution in the way in which he promoted, actively encouraged, and facilitated professional development for nurses at all levels. Damien's contribution in recent years has been his extensive experience in policy development in mental health care, with the development of audit outcomes and governance structures. This area of interest has seen the development of his interest in regulation and governance, with Damien developing a considerable body of expertise in the area of governance as it pertains to both mental health care and health care in general in Ireland.

VISION FOR YOUR LIFE'S WORK

Damien's vision is to complete his doctorate and to develop Bloomfield Health Services, with its established reputation, as a foremost centre for excellence for older persons' services, offering a wide range of inpatient and day services for both acute and continuing care requirements.

Damien describes himself as somebody who is driven, energetic, and an independent thinker. His decision-making is based on a combination of facts, a well-structured argument and the wider picture. He believes that a clear vision and objectives are important for decisions to be both coherent and transparent. He is not afraid to take risks, and encourages thinking outside the box. Damien emphasises the importance of clear team leadership, in which a vibrant, quality-driven, effective and efficient culture is nurtured, as it is key to the team achieving the best results in a person-centred health service. Central also to the team is imparting support, value, consistency and training to attain the level of service delivery required.

OTHER LEADERS WHO INFLUENCED YOU

People in leadership positions who influenced him were those at line manager and clinical nurse manager level, who worked with him when he was a Staff Nurse, and Directors of Nursing, Directors of Service and Chief Executives. Damien always observed their leadership skills and mirrored positive aspects of their leadership in his own development. This has assisted him in shaping his current leadership skills.

Outside of nursing, Feargal Quinn (an Irish Senator) is someone Damien has observed in terms of how he made his business so successful. From a health care perspective, business acumen is relevant in that the patient is a customer who is at the centre of what we do. This parallels Feargal Quinn's philosophy. Damien believes that Feargal Quinn has done this very successfully.

Damien encourages a mirroring of Quinn's successful communication skills, in the way in which we communicate with our patients and their families and provide a health care service of choice.

CHARACTERISTICS OF LEADERS

Damien believes that a leader needs to have a charismatic personality and a presence; be visionary; have an ability to see the practicalities necessary to deliver the plan; be willing to take the necessary risks; and combine these attributes with the ability to deliver. The ability to encourage and facilitate people to see the positives is also an important characteristic. A leader needs to be financially astute, a good planner, with attention to detail and an ability to deal with multiple activities but also to have the ability to deal with the unexpected crisis. The need to support the team is imperative to getting the job done. It is important to be fair and transparent in your dealings and not be afraid to bring people on to your team who will challenge thinking within that team so that development and growth continues.

SIGNIFICANT CHALLENGES

Damien has met many challenges over the years in his leadership role. One of the essential areas that requires continual focus is the need to encourage and facilitate clinical disciplines to work together towards a common goal of ensuring the delivery of person-centred care from a team that performs well together. He feels that there needs to be a greater awareness amongst individual disciplines, including nursing, of the need to cross-work at all times and to be able to understand each other's roles. The issue that often arises is the lack of understanding of the focus on the patient's need from a team approach as opposed to a unidisciplinary approach. While significant progress has been made in this area, work remains to be done.

He also believes that the ability to apply the team approach at organisational level to deliver the service that the patient requires is equally essential. He states that the blending of clinicians and nonclinicians in a team approach to service delivery within health care requires the closure of the gap to facilitate a greater understanding of the complementary roles and skills. This is paramount to ensure that that service delivery is of the highest quality and cost-effective.

OPPORTUNITIES THAT ENHANCED SUCCESS

Three key opportunities enhanced Damien's success: his appointment as Director of Nursing (2000); completing his MBA (2006); and his appointment as Chief Executive (2011).

His appointment as Director of Nursing gave him the opportunity to work at a senior level within an organisation and allowed him to demonstrate his ability to influence and shape a service. This allowed him to develop his department and to develop nursing as a profession, which was a significant stepping-stone for him, both personally and professionally. Completing an MBA gave him further diversification in terms of viewing nursing as an entity and then working toward influencing in a more meaningful way the greater organisation and service. His appointment to the position of Chief Executive has been a very positive move for Damien and has given him great scope in the further development of a service in totality with an exciting and positive future. This has enhanced the skills that he developed in his position as Head of Operations & Quality.

OBSTACLES ENCOUNTERED AND LESSONS LEARNED

Health care professions can demonstrate varying degrees of reticence regarding quality agendas delivered through accreditation processes and this has been an obstacle in moving forward. The achievements gained by an organisation can demonstrate the importance of information and feedback to a team. As the process developed, the team members saw the integral nature of quality in the day-to-day work and the positive achievements made when delivered well.

ADVICE TO ASPIRING LEADERS

Do not be afraid of hard work; be true to your own professional beliefs; be very clear about your vision; ensure you plan well; and have an acute awareness of the difference between being a manager and a leader. Seek out full information before making a final decision but be mindful of unexpected possibilities; know and grow your network; learn from your mistakes; be open, fair and transparent in your interactions; and be honest with yourself. Have clear expectations of others and be sure to communicate your expectations. Be mindful of, and flexible regarding, the bigger picture and have an awareness of organisational and wider politics and behaviours. Good emotional intelligence is an essential asset. Know your team's strengths and weaknesses. Be aware that hard work and commitment pays off.

CHAPTER 17
GERRY O'DWYER

Eileen Savage

Leaders need to be adept in seeking information beyond their comfort zone.

Gerry O'Dwyer is Regional Director of Operations of one of the four Health Service Executive (HSE) regions in Ireland: Dublin Mid Leinster. The role involves managing a range of health and personal social services provided by the HSE and its funded agencies, as well as managing the funding of services provided on behalf of the HSE through a large number of non-statutory agencies. The HSE Dublin Mid Leinster area spans a broad geographic region, including Longford, Westmeath, Laois, Offaly, Wicklow and South of the River Liffey. The large teaching hospitals in this region include Tallaght Hospital, St. James's Hospital, St. Vincent's University Hospital, the Royal Victoria Eye & Ear Hospital, two maternity hospitals and all the paediatric hospitals – Our Lady's Hospital for Sick Children, Crumlin; the Adelaide, Meath & National Children's Hospital (AMNCH) in Tallaght, as well as Temple Street Children's University Hospital – because of plans to amalgamate all children's hospitals into one National Children's Hospital. Prior to his current position, Gerry has held management positions as Chief Executive Officer of Our Lady's Hospital for Sick Children, Crumlin, and was Hospital Network Manager for HSE South. He is currently Vice President of the European Association of Hospital Managers (EAHM).

Gerry was born and grew up in Dublin with two siblings. He attended primary school in Drumcondra and later on the Navan Road. Secondary level education was at Carmelite College, Moate, Co. Westmeath, an all-boys boarding school. Gerry trained as a psychiatric nurse at St. Patrick's Psychiatric Hospital, St. James's Street, Dublin (now known as St. Patrick's University Hospital). He remained in psychiatric nursing services for a number of years, progressing through the nurse management grades to become Director of Nursing. Gerry worked in the Southern Health Board – Cork, and the South Eastern Health Board – Clonmel (both now part of HSE South). He went into mainstream management first as Service Manager, and then as Deputy General Manager/Deputy Chief Executive Officer at the Cork University Hospital Group. Gerry was one of a small number of health service managers in Ireland with a nursing background at that time.

EARLY INFLUENCES

Influenced by a teacher in secondary school, Gerry became a voluntary worker doing soup runs for the homeless with the Simon Community charity over a two-year period. Through this experience, Gerry was exposed to individuals who had mental health problems, some with a long history of mental illness and who were attending psychiatric services. He also met with individuals who were homeless and living rough. Having come from a relatively privileged and protected background, Gerry described his voluntary work as a formative experience, which motivated him to pursue a career in psychiatric nursing.

Once qualified as a psychiatric nurse, Gerry undertook a number of courses in counselling and management. A key influential person was a Director of Nursing (Ms Anne Kelly) at St. Patrick's Psychiatric Hospital, who challenged the *status quo* by appointing staff into senior positions on the basis of qualifications, experience and merit and not just on the basis of 'seniority'. Ms Kelly had leadership qualities and vision 'ahead of her time', which stamped the concept of integrated care on Gerry's mind. Gerry was strongly influenced also by a number of Directors of Nursing from both secular and religious orders with whom he worked over the years of his nursing career.

Other influences on Gerry's career were his parents, especially his mother who successfully ran a shop in a deprived area in Dublin's north inner city. Gerry's mother died when he was in his mid-twenties, following a long period of illness.

When growing up, and still to this day, Gerry has maintained his interest in Gaelic football and rugby. He also enjoys reading and following the media on international politics. Three renowned political leaders of international standing have influenced Gerry over time: Bill Clinton, 42nd President of the United States (1993 to 2001), who was a major supporter of the Northern Ireland peace process; Willie Brandt, Chancellor of the Federal Republic of Germany (1969 to 1974), who strived to achieve reconciliation between West Germany and the Soviet Bloc, and received a Nobel Peace Prize for his efforts; and Helmut Kohl, Chancellor of Germany (1982 to 1998), during which time he oversaw the re-unification of Germany. Gerry described these three men as very influential people and leaders who made enormous lifetime contributions and progress on political and social agendas. He described these three leaders as very good at gathering consensus to tackle and to resolve difficult political and societal issues. One of the hallmarks of the success of these men as leaders was that they had the capacity to influence communities of people, both within and outside their parent countries, to work towards goals and time-line targets, and they brought people with them all the way to achieve their targets and realise their goals. In some ways, the challenges faced by these political leaders in terms of reaching out to people, building relationships and gathering consensus across political and social divides resonates with the challenges faced by Regional Directors of Operations in the HSE, such as Gerry, within the context of major health service reform in Ireland over the past number of years; an agenda that remains a Government priority as set out in various strategy and policy documents, the most recent being *Future Health: a Strategic Framework for Reform of the Health Service 2012-2015.*

MAJOR LIFE EVENTS

Gerry's first appointment as a Director of Nursing was a major career event in terms of giving him the freedom to influence change in the services. He described his experiences of working in the mental health services in Cork and Clonmel. As a result of the roll-out of *Planning for the Future*, he was directly involved in the relocation of patients from psychiatric units to more appropriate settings. The move generated considerable, yet understandable, disquiet among all stakeholders. Although challenging, this experience provided Gerry with opportunities to influence change through negotiation, persuasion, people management and leadership. This experience strengthened Gerry's commitment and passion towards improving services, especially the need to have an integrated health service in this country.

CONTRIBUTION TO NURSING

When asked about his contribution to nursing, Gerry spoke of realising the leadership and management roles of nurses at executive and policy levels in the health services. In his management roles, his direct contribution to nursing has been to develop nurse managers as leaders in their own right towards improving services and supporting the change from the apprenticeship model to the university model of development. He spoke of his admiration for Professor Geraldine McCarthy,[7] who worked in Beaumont Hospital in the 1990s. Geraldine's role in management was 'phenomenal' and she was one of the first nurses in Ireland to 'break the mould' by taking up a senior development management position outside the traditional nursing line. Prior to this, most nurses pursuing careers in management generally stayed in positions within the nursing profession. The opportunity to influence the wider reform and improvement of services was realisable through the advancement of nurses across previously uncharted territory.

VISION FOR YOUR LIFE'S WORK

A seamless and integrated health service and inter-agency co-operation across State departments represents the core of Gerry's vision for his life's work. He spoke of being at the forefront of driving an agenda for a more integrated health service. He recalled his earlier experiences as a regional manager being marked by a very fragmented health service with little integration whatsoever. Since then, Gerry has been involved in major changes in reconfiguring health services within his area of responsibility. At national level, he has input into the process for determining the soon-to-be-announced hospital groups, as part of the implementation of *Future Health*.

Gerry has a vision for an economic model of healthcare in Ireland that takes account of quality, effectiveness, costs and outcomes. To this end, he is a fervent advocate of the need to clearly delineate and separate the role of commissioner and monitor of health services from the direct provider of health and personal social services. In Northern Ireland and the UK, for example, a commissioner determines the services needed and the health service provider is required to deliver the services purchased. This model ensures quality, equal access and good governance in public health services.

---

[7]   **Chapter 15**, *Leadership in Action: Influential Irish Women Nurses' Contribution to Society*, Geraldine McCarthy & Joyce J. Fitzpatrick, Oak Tree Press, 2012.

COMPETENCIES, STRENGTHS AND VALUES

A core competency of leaders is that they must demonstrate capacity to influence a vision for change or reform, and in doing so, encourage and bring people with them to realise this vision. People management, developing consensus and shared directions among people are critical to effective leadership. Persistence, political awareness, and exposing oneself to different and complex environments are strengths needed in leadership positions, especially within the context of health care reform, which can be fraught with conflicting agendas and power struggles at all levels.

According to Gerry, values inherent to his leadership concerning health care reform are quality and excellence in service provision and value for money. Good leadership is widely regarded as being central to the delivery of effective health care. In Gerry's experience, where care services have significant leadership from clinicians, they deliver far better results in terms of clinical effectiveness, patient safety, patient outcomes and financial management.

CHARACTERISTICS OF LEADERS

Leaders are good listeners and communicators with the capacity to gather consensus in tackling difficult issues. Effective leaders genuinely subscribe to a working agenda for reform and transformation. Additional characteristics of leaders are that they are questioning and inquiring in ways that allow in-depth analysis of and clarity of thought on the pros and cons of various arguments or agendas put forward for change. These characteristics provide leaders with a solid base and an intelligence that inspires confidence in individuals and communities of people to embrace change and reform.

SIGNIFICANT CHALLENGES

One of the problems with the Irish health care services is that there is a need for consensus and, although the social partnership process commenced almost 20 years ago and has been very good for the Irish economy, some opportunities were missed in the early days to integrate services in the interests of the patient. Since the abolition of the Health Boards and the subsequent transitions, significant change is now underway to reconfigure services; inroads are being made in this area with the advent of the Clinical care programmes and, particularly, the Acute Medicine Programme. Greater emphasis is placed on quality and patient safety and governance arrangements support this approach. In addition, there is greater service user involvement in every aspect of health service development.

Health care reform that involves reconfiguration and integration of services can be emotionally and politically charged, meeting resistance at all levels. This resistance poses significant challenges in bringing about change, which can take time, personal effort and energy.

Developing a mind-set of 'value for money' has become an important dimension of the delivery of public sector health services in Ireland. A fundamental question that we all should be asking is: "Are we providing value for money in the delivery of services?". Gerry's response to this is that clearly "we should be" and that our focus should be on maximising every euro of taxpayers' money for the betterment of public health. He noted that the health services in the public sector could learn from some of the operational practices in the private sector.

OPPORTUNITIES THAT ENHANCED SUCCESS

Gerry described the opportunity of progressing 'up the ladder' in management through an apprenticeship model as enhancing his success in becoming a Regional Director of Operations in the HSE. This provided Gerry with insights into managing people and services at various levels of organisational complexity. He spoke of embracing opportunities as they arise or indeed seeking out new opportunities. Throughout his working life, Gerry has never spent more than a short number of years in any one post, or indeed in any one area. Gerry noted that it was difficult at times for his family moving house and location but that they now reflect on the richness of experiencing change and different environments. He spoke fondly of the support of his wife, who believed that "in order to be a leader and in order to work at the highest level, you need exposure to different environments and then to move to new challenges". Gerry endorsed this view and noted that, in a successful business worldwide, the need for turnover is seen as vital for renewal and innovation.

ADVICE TO ASPIRING LEADERS

Leaders need to very clearly understand the work that they are undertaking because their perceptions of what this work might involve can differ substantially from what it really involves. A thorough 'reconnaissance' is important for aspiring leaders to skill themselves up for the 'known and unknown'. In other words, they need to be adept at seeking information and developing relationships and competencies beyond their comfort zone and familiar environments with a view to analysing a range of forces that may impact on their work and leadership aspirations.

Communication skills are essential. Good listening is critical. It is necessary for a leader to develop the capacity to pick up on the verbal and non-verbal cues of people that they wish to lead. There is a need for a clear vision consistent with what policy-makers want and an understanding of the parameters to be achieved. Embedding the cultural capabilities espoused by Future health will require strong leadership at clinical, senior managerial – and critically – frontline management level.

CHAPTER 18
MICHAEL SHANNON

Mary Ellen Gerardina Harnett-Collins

Political astuteness is an absolute imperative.

Michael Shannon is Director of the Office for Nursing & Midwifery Services in the Health Service Executive (HSE) since 2011. This Office provides leadership, supports excellence and innovation and builds capacity in nursing and midwifery to enhance patient care and service. Michael worked in the Department of Health for three years as a Nurse Advisor with Peta

Taaffe,[8] who was Ireland's first Chief Nurse. He has worked as Director of Nursing at Letterkenny Hospital and at Sligo General Hospital and Hospice before working with the Nursing & Midwifery Planning & Development Unit in HSE Dublin Mid-Leinster. Michael holds a BSc from Coleraine University; a Diploma in Pharmacology from the Royal College of Surgeons in Ireland; a Master's in Business Administration in Health Studies from the Michael Smurfit Graduate School of Business at University College Dublin; and he recently completed a PhD focused on how skill mix is characterised in Irish acute hospitals.

EARLY INFLUENCES

Michael Shannon was born in Coventry, England and is the second-eldest of five. His older sister, Elizabeth, is a midwife who runs a private practice in England. His only brother, Joseph, is an executive chef in Sligo and features on TV3. His sister Bernadette lives in Ireland and is a business entrepreneur, while his other sister Dolores is a nurse who works for a voluntary organisation providing work placement opportunities for clients. His father, also Michael, was a renowned musician and his mother Mary, who has passed away, was also a nurse. She was a quiet country woman, who sought no accolades but focused on helping others, always upholding principles of respect for others. She worked on night duty in the care of older people and was a tremendous influence on Michael. His great-aunt Ellen, who was a teacher, is described as an inspirational professional woman.

Michael's formative years were spent in Coventry and at age 11, the family returned to Enniscrone, Co. Sligo, where he attended a mixed-gender secondary school run by a religious order. Michael spoke of his great admiration for the progressiveness of the nuns in the context of exposing students to public speaking, music, art, debating – far more than just the traditional subjects of secondary school. From the age of 13, Michael worked in different positions in diverse places such as cafés and hospitals, shaping his resilience and work ethos. Michael expresses fond memories of that time.

---

[8]   **Chapter 21**, *Leadership in Action: Influential Irish Women Nurses' Contribution to Society*, Geraldine McCarthy & Joyce J. Fitzpatrick, Oak Tree Press, 2012.

He completed the Leaving Certificate in 1981. Elizabeth, his sister, had gone to Northern Ireland to train as a nurse, contributing to a sense of excitement for Michael's own future. A presentation on nursing as a career given by the Principal Tutor for Sligo General Hospital (Joe Mullen) was another significant influence. Though he considered university, Michael did not want to put his family through that financial burden in the early 1980s, so he began training as a general nurse in 1981 at Sligo General Hospital with one other man and 14 women. His reflections on this time are very good.

Michael then commenced mental health nurse training at St. John of God Hospital in Stilorgan, Dublin. There he began a journey in search of answers relating to mental health service provision and institutionalisation, as well as the social dilemmas that presented for those with mental illness. He became a member of a group of 10 specialising in alcohol misuse and psychotic disorders. Michael was introduced to care planning, models of nursing and the application of information technology for health purposes. Mrs Graham, the Director of Nursing of St. John of God at the time, influenced Michael. She had a sense of responsibility, was firm but kind, valued staff, and had a very good patient caring ethos. Michael staffed there for six months before taking a post as Staff Nurse at Baggot Street Hospital, Dublin. With good mentorship, including that from the then Matron (Peta Taaffe), and guidance mixed with a personal hunger for good patient care, Michael thrived in the cardio-thoracic ward. Michael describes Peta Taaffe as a remarkable, pragmatic, able and empowering woman. She had a presence and a passion for patient care, and remarkable political discernment.

Rationalisation of Dublin hospitals meant a transfer to St. James's Hospital but Michael opted to return to Sligo, where he worked for a year in orthopaedics and surgery, subsequently undertaking an orthopaedic course in Coventry, where he graduated in 1989 with an English National Board qualification. Teaching and learning within this course was centred on care planning and it was during this time that Michael was exposed to skill mix, which has become a lifetime academic and practice interest.

Michael staffed in Intensive Care and moved from there to a Charge Nurse post in St. Mary's, Paddington in London and was influenced there by a Senior Charge Nurse. She consistently demonstrated professionalism, gained widespread respect and had organisational abilities; she was efficient, regardless of resources, and prioritised patient care. Subsequently, Michael accepted the position of Charge Nurse in orthopaedics in Letterkenny Hospital. The leadership programme offered by the Office for Health Management in 1998 equipped him with competencies in leadership, political awareness, and networking.

MAJOR LIFE EVENTS

Michael did not actively plan his career, but believes that he was often in the right place at the right time. People, economy and providence shaped Michael's career path. Moving from Ireland to England was a significant life experience both as a child and adult. He remembers the Victoria train station bombings in London, being Irish, the horror of the bombs, yet being part of caring for the sick. The cultural issues of being Irish and working in England at that time contributed to a deep cultural understanding and learning.

Michael describes his experience of volunteering with the Samaritans as a major positive life event. The Samaritans' ethos and how they train, support, and value their volunteers has been influential.

Michael reflects on negative life experiences and the consequences of poor leadership. On one of his first days in a clinical environment, he was commanded by the ward charge nurse to 'go feed that patient'. Unbeknownst to Michael, the patient had passed away. This nurse subsequently suggested that Michael killed this man as a consequence of feeding him. He has never forgotten the callousness he experienced; she was pivotal to that ward and people hated working there. Similarly, he worked with a Director of Nursing who was a bully. In making a simple decision, it was like a Rubik cube in working out how she might react to any aspect of that decision; her influence was very negative over the environment. Nevertheless, as in every aspect of life, there was learning from these experiences.

VISION FOR YOUR LIFE'S WORK

Michael expresses his belief in nursing and nursing's capacity to support society. His vision is to develop nursing and midwifery potential, based on care, compassion and safety, facilitated by a much wider scope of practice. He advocates for the on-going development of care and respect within the profession. He sees the Directors of Nursing as enabling this goal and his vision is to support the Directors and their teams in partnership with education, regulation and policy. Michael envisages 'a leaner profession', more autonomous, less bureaucratic, having greater clarity, and the authority to make decisions at the point of care. He advocates for a much greater contribution by nurses and midwives to a more expansive health policy.

COMPETENCIES, STRENGTHS AND VALUES

Michael says he is a good facilitator and an attentive listener. Team-working is a strength, and he highlights the concept of personal responsibility of all team members and accountability for individual and team performance. Leadership is a personal skill Michael holds, stating that democracy is important in empowering people to fulfil their roles. He advocates a situational leadership style in achieving the patient's best interest in care.

CHARACTERISTICS OF LEADERS

Having passion for what you believe in; managing people appropriately; having political astuteness; knowing who the key players are; being able to influence and negotiate are important characteristics. The ability to take risks; charisma and presence; and having a leader supporting you or coaching you are important.

SIGNIFICANT CHALLENGES

A significant challenge is the articulation of the profession's worth and value. This is particularly important in certain care environments such as intellectual disability nursing and in Advanced Nursing Practice, where some propose physician assistants as an alternative. Ensuring graduates are allowed to use and advance their capabilities in maximising patient care is a challenge. Re-focusing on clinical leadership within the context of skill mix; the need to own and retrieve management of everything that comes or goes through the ward or community area; health policy and ensuring the profession is fit for purpose within a universal health care model; integrating practice, academia and policy; and leadership of the profession are significant challenges.

OPPORTUNITIES THAT ENHANCED SUCCESS

Working with people who believed in him and taking risks enhanced Michael's success. Working abroad created opportunities that were not always available in Ireland. Career development was achieved as opportunities arose and encouragement of others played a part. Working within the policy division of the Department of Health also enhanced his success.

OBSTACLES ENCOUNTERED AND LESSONS LEARNED

Michael suggests that some obstacles have come from professional colleagues where a unified voice is not always present. He acknowledges the role of unions; however, he advocates that this should not be the only voice heard. Nurses and midwives work in a very bureaucratic environment, where sometimes decisions are not made but should be made at the appropriate level of responsibility. Nurses need to overcome obstacles and take ownership of their roles within the context of individual, family and community care environments. There should be a much stronger nursing profession from a leadership perspective.

ADVICE TO ASPIRING LEADERS

Believe in yourself; have passion for what you do; think about your purpose; think of the bigger picture and your destination; take risks; network; and know those who exert power and influence in the HSE. Develop the team you are working with, believe in your team and trust them and be honest. Have a vision and a strategy for your destination. Be visible but also be assertive and honest regarding what you can and cannot do. Enjoy life outside of work; have a good support system; make sure you build in some quality time for yourself. Professionally develop yourself; know who you can trust; get a coach or similar form of support.

CHAPTER 19
FATHER RAYMOND SWEENEY

Elizabeth Weathers

Let the hare sit.

Father Raymond Sweeney was born in Loughrea, Co. Galway in 1953. He is the youngest of a family of five and is a half-twin. His parents were Dermot and Bridget Sweeney. Raymond attended the local National School in Loughrea and went to St. Brigid's Vocational School, where he sat his Leaving Certificate. Upon completion of this, he wanted to join a religious order but was advised by a schoolteacher to apply to St. Patrick's College,

Maynooth and to join the priesthood. He spent time in St. Patrick's College, where he completed a Diploma in Philosophy, before travelling to Rome to study theology. In Rome, Raymond joined the Cistercians, an enclosed Roman Catholic order, but was encouraged to leave his priesthood studies and instead to choose a profession.

He worked in different organisations, including the Candle Community Trust in Ballyfermot, Dublin, where he was employed as a youth worker for two years. In 1983, he began his psychiatric nursing training in St. Vincent's Hospital in Fairview, Dublin. Thereafter, Raymond was employed as a Staff Nurse in St. Vincent's Hospital and in 1987, he commenced his general nurse training in Richmond Hospital, Dublin, which in 1990 became part of Beaumont Hospital. Raymond worked in Beaumont for eight years. During this time, he also worked part-time at the National Drug Treatment Centre in Pearse Street, Dublin. Raymond worked in the Central Mental Hospital, Dundrum from 1996 to 2002 and progressed from Charge Nurse to Assistant Director of Nursing to Director of Nursing. From 2002 to 2008, he was Director of Nursing at St. Brigid's Hospital, Ballinasloe, Co. Galway, where the East Galway Mental Health Services was based. He was ordained a Catholic priest in June 2011 and is now based in the parish of Portumna. He holds a Diploma in Psychiatric Nursing (St. Vincent's Hospital, 1986); a Diploma in General Nursing (St. Laurence's/Beaumont Hospital, 1988); a BA in Healthcare Management (Institute of Public Administration, 1993); a MA in Healthcare Management (Dublin City University, 1998); a Bachelor of Law degree (National University of Ireland, Galway, 2006); and a Master of Law degree (National University of Ireland, Galway, 2007). Raymond commenced a PhD in Law at the National University of Ireland Galway in January 2012.

EARLY INFLUENCES

From a personal perspective, Raymond cites his mother as a major influence in his life. Bridget was a midwife in Loughrea before becoming a district nurse and then a public health nurse. Raymond describes her as a very compassionate person who cared about other people. From a professional perspective, Raymond cites Professor Geraldine McCarthy[9] as a major influence. Working with her in Beaumont from 1990 to 1993 opened doors and windows in his mind that he had never even imagined. Nurse Tutors, in particular Sister Nuala Dolan, Evelyn Ryan (St. Vincent's Hospital), and Annette Donnollan (Richmond/Beaumont Hospital) were influential. Raymond undertook several courses in psychotherapy and transpersonal psychology at the Institute of Psycho-synthesis. The Director of the Institute, Father Michael O'Regan, was also influential.

MAJOR LIFE EVENTS

Raymond acknowledges that there have been many events in his life that have shaped who he is today. He mentions the experience of growing up and some mistakes he made. However, he says the important thing is that he has learnt from these mistakes by picking himself up and moving on. Raymond also describes how he has learned to own his own humanity and love himself. Yet this can be difficult in modern society where there is little respect for humanity and privacy. Raymond refers especially to the media in which people's privacy is often exploited to provide entertainment. Furthermore, Raymond says that as a priest, he is privy to people's lives and the pain that people experience, which makes him more aware of the importance of privacy.

Raymond speaks of the importance of accepting oneself in spite of any 'baggage' – positive or negative life experiences. Some experiences that he has had have made him aware of his individuality and, in some ways, his isolation in life. Raymond mentions death as also being a life-changing event, especially the death of a family member, which changes the family dynamics. However, he says that the important thing is how you can integrate these changes into your life and how you mind yourself through such events. In Raymond's opinion, all human beings need to seek supervision and support in life when necessary.

---

[9]   **Chapter 15**, *Leadership in Action: Influential Irish Women Nurses' Contribution to Society*, Geraldine McCarthy & Joyce J. Fitzpatrick, Oak Tree Press, 2012.

CONTRIBUTION TO NURSING

Raymond believes one of his major contributions was facilitating the development of others and promoting a service that allowed people to be proud of what they are doing. He has always encouraged staff to continue with their professional development and never had a problem granting time off for education. During his time in the Central Mental Hospital, Dundrum, he organised multidisciplinary conferences, which enhanced morale amongst staff. He says that, from a management perspective, it is about treating people with humanity and respect.

Raymond always searched for opportunities to care, for patients but also for staff. He considered this part of his role as a manager. For example, if a staff member was ever sick or bereaved, he would be sure to contact them or send them a card to make sure they were all right. This management style was an important contribution to nursing and created a culture of compassionate care.

Throughout his career, Raymond has tried to promote three prominent values: compassion, respect and safety. He believes it was when he worked in Dundrum that he really began to articulate these values by first creating a compassionate and caring environment for staff and patients. He believes that nobody is entitled to respect – it is something that must be earned. He maintains that, if you treat people with respect, then you will be respected in return. Safety also has been to the forefront throughout Raymond's career, especially in management. In his opinion, safety of both patients and staff is pivotal. One of Raymond's major contributions in this regard was developing policies for safe practice and the introduction of documentation policies. Raymond emphasises the importance of having systems in place that help to ensure safety.

VISION FOR YOUR LIFE'S WORK

Raymond hopes that nursing does not lose its humanity but also that it remains professional. He highlights the importance of valuing people, not only in monetary terms but also in human terms. Raymond also would like to see nurses valuing their own contribution to health care. He believes that the future for nursing lies in continuing education for nurses. Nurses need to be motivated in this regard, as well as being facilitated to partake in further education.

Raymond mentions the importance of ensuring a high standard of mental health service. He maintains that the introduction of primary care teams is vital and that these teams should include nurse counsellors. Raymond notes that psychiatry deals with the major mental illnesses such as chronic depression and psychosis but there is also a need to address the 'worried well' who need more than medication.

From a personal perspective, Raymond feels very privileged to be a priest. It allows him the opportunity to care for families in a very special way but it can be challenging at times. He would like to see some changes within the Catholic Church: it needs to regard itself as a profession and learn from systems that exist in other professions. Raymond feels that all priests should be trained in the area of pastoral and spiritual supervision. He believes this would allow priests to provide further psychological support to people. The Church should be about helping people and nobody should be isolated in the church. Furthermore, Raymond identifies the need for more ownership by the laity of the church, which will entail a release of ownership by priests. In his opinion, there is a wealth of care, spirituality, mysticism and love in the church that is sometimes buried under institutional issues. Everybody is invited to have a personal relationship with God but the institution sometimes clouds the relationship.

COMPETENCIES, STRENGTHS AND VALUES

Raymond says that education has enabled him to achieve competence in both his career and personal life. He has learned about the importance of systems that ensure safety and reduce error. Raymond highlights the need for solid research-based systems, especially within healthcare. He likes the boundaries created by systems without being too restrictive.

Raymond describes himself as an organised person who always likes to be prepared. For example, he likes to spend time preparing for a homily and putting thought into it. He credits these skills to his time as Research Assistant with Professor Geraldine McCarthy. Organising the multidisciplinary conferences in Dundrum and Ballinasloe are examples of when Raymond made good use of these skills.

Raymond remembers a skill he acquired from his time in the Cistercian monastery: how to cut hair. This proved very useful to him in Dundrum, where it allowed him to engage with patients on a one-to-one basis, to build rapport gain trust, and make a difference.

CHARACTERISTICS OF LEADERS

Compassion, respect, safety, ensuring the dignity and privacy of other people, and being there for staff and patients are important characteristics. Do not misuse power or employ a dictatorship style of management. Good leadership can be achieved without 'cracking the whip'. Raymond cites Joe McFadden, former Director of Nursing in the Central Mental Hospital, Dundrum as a person who exemplified good leadership and a learned wisdom. Joe had a saying: "Let the hare sit", because when the hare is sitting you don't have to shoot it! In other words, having that intuitive sense to hold back a little and not react to everything is a very important characteristic of a leader.

A good leader will never lose perspective. Communication and the ability to negotiate with, for example, the trade unions is an important aspect of leadership. Regular meetings with staff, to discuss any issues, eliminate the 'them and us' barrier is one way of building rapport and ensuring transparency. Have openness in communication.

Be prepared for the isolation associated with being a leader. Leaders need to make difficult decisions sometimes and cannot please everyone. As a leader, you must deal with human conflicts, jealousies and resentments.

SIGNIFICANT CHALLENGES

Raymond was faced with many challenges throughout his personal and professional life. One significant professional challenge was trying to begin nursing training. Sometimes, he felt discriminated against from gender and age perspectives. He remembers being told that he would not be able for the coursework in nursing because he was over the age of 27. However, Raymond acknowledges that things have changed since the 1980s and now there are increasing numbers of men in nursing.

Another professional challenge was his role in change management, especially in the Central Mental Hospital, Dundrum and in the East Galway Mental Health Services. For example, his role in the introduction of documentation and policies in Dundrum was a major change at the time, as was managing the change from an institution to a community-based approach in the Mental Health Services. Raymond also refers to the challenge of promoting a professional nursing culture and the promotion of education.

OPPORTUNITIES THAT ENHANCED SUCCESS

Raymond feels that the education he undertook enhanced every professional opportunity. He believes that he gained a better understanding of health and health care through education. For Raymond, studying in the priesthood and in the monastery gave him a certain understanding of spiritual life. His experiences in life have taught him to focus on the person always and to see beyond the faults. Raymond admits there was a time when he lacked self-confidence and describes some difficult life experiences.

Raymond credits his experiences in the church and in nursing as opportunities that made him who he is today. For example, he is more sensitive towards other people and always considers the person beneath any outwardly faults or appearances. He now realises how past experiences have brought meaning to his life.

OBSTACLES ENCOUNTERED AND LESSONS LEARNED

Raymond can identify numerous obstacles that he encountered. The most prominent would have been the gender and age discrimination he had to face at times in his nursing career. Also, as a manager, Raymond found some of the issues that arose difficult to resolve and he had to consider many perspectives: the staff, the unions, and management boards. Raymond found environmental and cultural challenges within the health care system. Raymond tried to compromise and work with people. An important lesson he learned was to deal with issues as they arise, which includes minor issues.

In Raymond's experience of management, he has encountered people of all backgrounds, values and cultures. He came across people who had personal problems that were impacting on their work. He learned the importance of addressing these personal problems and supporting people through them. Furthermore, he has learned that appearances can be very deceptive – a person may appear happy and healthy at work but actually may have underlying problems in their personal life.

ADVICE TO ASPIRING LEADERS

Raymond's advice to leaders is to mind yourself, and to seek supervision and support from others. Listen to yourself and make time for self-reflection; this will prevent burnout. Do your best with what you have in a difficult economic climate and remember the values of compassion, respect, and safety.

CHAPTER 20
JOE WOLFE

Alice Coffey

Nothing beats preparation, focus and hard work, and if you are determined enough to do something, you will succeed.

Joe Wolfe is Director of the Wolfe Group, a company specialising in Quality and Audit, Training and Organisational Development in health and social care organisations. Joe has acted as external consultant to the Mental Health Commission, the National Disability Authority and the Health Research Board and has worked with many statutory bodies and voluntary agencies to support quality improvement and development. He and his team have been instrumental in the development and implementation of National Quality Standards. Joe trained in intellectual disability nursing with the Hospitaller Order of St. John of God, in St. Mary's, Drumcar, in Co. Louth and completed a postgraduate qualification in mental health nursing in the St. John of God Hospital in Stilorgan, Dublin. Joe worked in the United Kingdom (UK) in a number of different management positions in various services before progressing to the post of Clinical Nurse Specialist/Senior Manager with Parkside Healthcare in London in the early 1990s. He completed a Master's degree in Mental Health Interventions, a qualification in teaching and assessing and a qualification in quality assurance. Joe returned to Ireland in 1996, at 28 years of age, to take up a position of Director of Nursing & Allied Services with the Irish Sisters of Charity and, after a number of years, decided that there was a need for an independent organisation to assist health and social care services to improve and develop. Since then the Wolfe Group has conducted in excess of 300 audits and independent evaluations across the health and social care sector, has trained many thousands of staff in skills-based training programmes and has supported mental health services, older person's services, children's services, acute hospitals and services for people with disabilities to improve and develop.

EARLY INFLUENCES

Joe was born in Cork city and came third in a family of seven children. His mother worked at the Cope Foundation, a service for children and adults with intellectual disability in Cork city. While still at school (at age 16), Joe volunteered to work at Cope Foundation and developed a real interest in working with people who had a profound disability. He knew then that he wanted his career to be in nursing. Joe describes his parents as being very strong influences in his early years, particularly in their support of him in his career choices.

His early training as a nurse, particularly his education in Stilorgan, was a key influence in his career. Individuals such as Briege O'Neill (Nurse Tutor) and Mary Coyne and Margaret Cotter

(Clinical Teachers) are remembered especially for their positive impact on his learning and development in his intellectual disability training. Briege, according to Joe was an inspirational leader and mentor. She was an extremely good communicator and had a passion for nursing. Mary Coyne and Margaret Cotter had excellent technical and practical skills and were very supportive of students. They were different individuals but were influential. What stood out in all of these influential people was the combination of skill, knowledge and passion for the profession.

Joe states that his wife, Nicola, has been his greatest influence and supporter throughout his career. Nicola is also a Registered Nurse in Intellectual Disability & Mental Health, a former Nurse Tutor and together with Joe, is co-director of the Wolfe Group.

While in the UK, and studying for his Master's degree, two great influences on Joe's learning and development were Professor Kevin Gournay OBE and Dr Joanna Bennett. Professor Gournay developed the Master's programme (MSc in Mental Health Interventions) at Middlesex University in London and Dr. Bennett was a lecturer on the programme. The Master's programme, the first of its kind at the time, was skills-based and very rigorous and interactive. Both of these individuals were inspirational, personable and passionate about developing nursing as a strong profession. Professor Gournay was a 'trail blazer', the first nurse to become Professor of the Institute of Psychiatry in London, and he was a very successful Head of Research at the Institute. Professor Gournay is now retired but remains active in development work internationally and is a prolific writer. Joe remains in contact, working with Professor Gournay on a number of projects over the last few years.

MAJOR LIFE EVENTS

About five years ago, Joe personally experienced the Irish health services and saw the services from the other side. This was a major event in his life and a major learning curve. It was obvious from this experience that quality was not consistent across services, either from a clinical or a standards perspective. As a result, Joe has a very different perspective of health services and clinical practice and he is firmly of the view that, while good practice must be affirmed and acknowledged, services must reach national standards, address poor and unacceptable practices and not tolerate professionals who clearly flout or are just unable to meet the high standards of care that we are obliged to provide.

CONTRIBUTION TO NURSING

Although Joe is not now involved in direct patient care, he feels that he is more involved in nursing practice than ever. He spends at least three days per week in one service or another, evaluating the service, reporting, developing improvement plans and training staff around the country. Joe feels that the Wolfe Group is at the heart of the health and social services all the time, supporting services to improve quality.

According to Joe, his nursing education has contributed greatly to the success of his career in organisational development. Joe says that nurses have well-developed communication and organisational skills, empathy and management skills that have been shaped through training. Joe feels that the more one moves around the services and experiences different views of care and service provision, the more one has to offer. A background in nursing provides one with credibility.

Within the Wolfe Group, Joe has contributed directly to the development of standards in care and services and has seen significant positive changes over the years. With his team, he has prepared organisations for inspection by the Health Information & Quality Authority and has published works promoting quality systems and person-centred service development. The group have produced detailed scientific reports and a range of audit and evaluation tools to support these developments.

VISION FOR YOUR LIFE'S WORK

Joe's vision for his life's work is focused on influencing the improvement in the quality of health and social services in Ireland. He hopes to improve the person's experiences of these services and develop the knowledge and skills of staff and the competency of management in health and social care services.

COMPETENCIES, STRENGTHS AND VALUES

Joe described his strengths in organisation, communication and in influencing people as being paramount to being a good leader. He also describes himself as a 'completer/finisher' and says this trait is essential when undertaking an organisational improvement or development project. Joe considers that his competencies in undertaking research and in writing are of particular importance to his role in quality improvement and organisational development. For a leader, the ability to clearly articulate ideas and vision is crucial.

Joe strongly believes that one should always treat people as you would want yourself or a member of your family to be treated and individuals should strive to deliver care at the highest possible standard at all times.

OTHER LEADERS THAT INFLUENCED YOU

The leadership influences in Joe's earlier career as a student nurse in Ireland, and as a Clinical Nurse Specialist and as a Clinical Manager in the UK, were very positive. The leaders concerned were inspirational, progressive, and passionate about their profession and supported him in his education and development. He had a number of excellent mentors, both in education and in clinical practice with whom he maintains contact.

In contrast, there were a small number of individuals in leadership positions throughout his career that Joe learned not to follow. These individuals were dogmatic, had a dictatorial style of leadership, were not open to discussion and undermined others. Some appeared to be very professional, but were not focused on the needs of the service users. His experiences of this type of leadership assisted Joe in identifying traits of leadership that he did not wish to attain. He viewed these experiences as valuable learning and uses them as examples of poor leadership in his teaching today.

CHARACTERISTICS OF LEADERS

Joe describes a good leader as someone who is genuine, authentic and believes in what they are doing. People want to support a good leader, rather than just follow. Good leaders in nursing need to be able to manage and to bring people along with them. They need to be excellent communicators and to instil a passion for quality services. They need to be empathic, to have strong influencing skills and to be fair and just.

SIGNIFICANT CHALLENGES

There are a number of challenges presently in nursing but what is mainly missing in the development of leadership in nursing is mentorship. Mentoring and shaping of individuals for their role in leadership and management is most important. If we do not get this right, according to Joe, we are rudderless. At every level in our nursing career, we need mentorship to bring us to our next level of competency. Joe has worked with a number of nurses in senior management positions who never had anyone to mentor or help them shape their careers. Joe remembers hearing one Director of Nursing, who was close to retirement, stating to him, "I never got any feedback on how I was doing, even as a Director of Nursing, but I must have been doing something right because I was never told that I was doing things wrong". Joe uses this quote to illustrate that many nurses in leadership positions in the past had been given little direction or feedback/mentoring. Nurses need to be mentored and supported in their development, so that the profession has effective and inspirational leaders for the future.

OPPORTUNITIES THAT ENHANCED SUCCESS

There were few career opportunities for nurses in Ireland when Joe first qualified. However, a number of opportunities arose once he moved to the UK. The opportunity to work in a combined career as a clinical nurse specialist, researcher and manager in mental health services provided challenges and learning opportunities that prepared him for his future career in the business of training and development. Joe is very grateful to have had the opportunity to work with, and learn from, very passionate and influential people in clinical practice, education and management. The support and encouragement he received provided him with the competence to identify service needs and the confidence to set up his business.

Education certainly made a huge difference. Postgraduate studies, particularly the Master's degree, helped in securing promotion. Postgraduate education, coupled with the breadth of experience he gained in the UK, also made it easier to succeed in his career when Joe returned to Ireland.

OBSTACLES ENCOUNTERED AND LESSONS LEARNED

In the past in Ireland, the main obstacles for nurses such as Joe were lack of educational opportunities, academic development and lack of clarity and opportunities regarding career progression. The opportunities are far greater for nurses now than when Joe qualified as a nurse. So many successful leaders in business were first trained as nurses and this shows the degree of expertise that nurses possess. According to Joe, the way forward for nurses who want to progress is always to determine what you want to do, determine what skills and training you need to achieve and to go and get these.

ADVICE TO ASPIRING LEADERS

Identify where you want to go, the competencies you require to get there and gain those competencies through targeted education and training. Get experience, travel and see services elsewhere and learn from them. Push yourself outside your comfort zone. Take opportunities as they come and continue to build on your experience. Find people with a similar mind-set to support and mentor you. As a leader, see the potential in others, help them identify their strengths and areas for development and shape and mentor them to become great managers and leaders.

CHAPTER 21
LESSONS LEARNED: PREPARING FUTURE LEADERS

Geraldine McCarthy and Joyce J. Fitzpatrick

This book consists of 19 interviews with men in leadership positions who began their careers as nurses. Some have diversified and now lead important academic, health, social or entrepreneurial enterprises. In Ireland, nursing education and the health service has changed considerably since 2000. Three Professors of Nursing and one Professor of Midwifery are profiled. In addition, descriptions are given of the work done by men who have taken key roles in organisations and clinical practice.

Each interview was conducted based on a format that included information on: early influences; major life events; vision for life's work; competencies, strengths, and values; characteristics of leaders; significant challenges; opportunities that enhanced success; and advice to aspiring leaders. In the following paragraphs, we merge the information gathered to provide an overview of these key elements across interviews.

Early influences included those of parents who believed in education and professional careers for all family members. The necessity to earn a living and have constant employment was also an influencing factor. Siblings, friends, neighbours and work colleagues who encouraged were important. Teachers with high standards and high expectations and nurses with expertise in communication, management and clinical ability were identified as influential. People who were trustful and those who listened and were attentive to aspirations were particularly important.

Major life events were parents' or siblings' deaths, working abroad and associated cultural experiences. Other events identified by the men leaders were related to early nursing experiences, including challenges that helped them to discover their talents and abilities. Opportunities to represent nurses on a variety of governing bodies at various organisational and community levels were particularly influential.

Vision for life's work was to contribute to society, to give of oneself, including supporting others through a wide range of professional and personal activities. These core values permeated all participants' vision for their work. There was also an intention to deliver and manage service in a quality and safe manner. There was a belief in teams and the fact that one cannot work alone but rather one needs the support and involvement of other individuals. There was an emphasis on the fact that people have to learn and cope with failure, be ready and available for opportunities as they are presented and treat all people and situations on their own merits.

Competencies, strengths and values held by individuals across interviews can be summed up as having resilience, fairness, openness, ability to listen, willingness to learn and to work hard. Team-building, ethical stance, fact-selecting, decision-making, risk-taking, valuing others while recognising failures, but intolerance to inefficiencies and laziness were profiled. The ability to learn and listen, to thoroughly investigate situations, to be widely read, intelligent, courageous, a good communicator and well-organised were important. Competencies also included a commitment to the devolvement of authority, an ability to step into the unknown and to make unpopular decisions when needed.

Leader characteristics that were perceived as important included: being fair; non-judgemental; a strategic thinker; visionary; reflective; positive; challenging; inspiring; instilling hope; using opportunities; and knowing your business. A belief in yourself and in what you are doing; in being courageous; well-organised; respectful and accommodating of the views of others; a team-builder; and bearing no grudges and the ability to move on after a disagreement also were important characteristics identified.

Significant challenges included being a man seeking entry into nursing and being employed as a nurse and operating in a female-dominated environment. Also achieving a work/life balance, experiencing personal illness, and direct clinical care involving traumatic situations were challenges. Time management, entrenched beliefs of other health care professionals, hierarchical structures, working towards accreditation and the provision of funding were particularly challenging.

Opportunities that enhanced success included being in the right place at the right time, having a good education, being able to travel, and having the ability to identify excellent mentors. Leaders also identified professional opportunities, especially promotional opportunities and membership on boards, involvement in strategic planning and being lucky to have trained as a nurse as key to their success.

Obstacles encountered related to working with people with diverse opinions; management of difficult people; situations where there was no obvious learning from mistakes; and inappropriately-trained people occupying posts. Not being listened to, a lack of vision among co-workers, and bureaucracy were also encountered.

Lessons learned and advice to aspiring leaders were as follows: distance yourself from the issue; express your opinions and give suggestions; let praise go to others if necessary; do not stand back; know yourself and what motivates you; look for opportunities where you can use your skills and competencies; be confident; have an ethical approach and be respectful of all people you encounter; be fair; find learning in rejection of your ideas; develop resilience; depersonalise issues; live a balanced life; commit to what you do; build teams and allocate work according to individual capacity; network outside your own discipline; educate yourself to the highest possible level and try to study with others, be well-researched; get a mentor, have a close friend; take risks; learn from failure; be political; be visible, organised, and flexible; use teams; do not expect people to be as enthusiastic as yourself; be an easy person to talk to; be non-judgemental; be caring. Many of these qualities are at the foundation of what was learned in nursing.

We hope in reading the stories that you will have learned about leadership and the influences on leadership. We want you to be energised and motivated in your career and wish that you would benchmark yourself against the experiences profiled and find it a beneficial exercise.

THE EDITORS

Geraldine McCarthy PhD MSN MEd DipN RNT RGN was founding Professor and Dean of the Catherine McAuley School of Nursing & Midwifery, which was established in University College Cork (UCC) in 1994. From 2010 to 2011, she held the post of Acting Head of the College of Medicine & Health at UCC, providing strategic leadership in research and educational programmes in  Medicine, Dentistry, Therapies, Pharmacy, Nursing and Midwifery.

She has held a variety of other positions in Ireland, the UK, USA and Canada. She holds a MEd from Trinity College Dublin (TCD), and MSN and PhD degrees in Nursing from Case Western Reserve University, Cleveland, Ohio, USA. She has been a member of a number of national and EU bodies, including the Commission on Nursing, the Nurse Education Forum, the Task Force on Undergraduate Medical Education and a Ministerial nominee to the Health Information & Quality Authority and to the Fulbright Commission.

She has published over 120 papers and has presented at national and international conferences. Her research interests include those associated with management and chronic disease self-care, especially in elderly care. She leads the Healthy Ageing Research Theme within the School and supervises both PhD and MSc students. In addition, she is a member of local Health Service Reconfiguration Team that is working to transform the Hospital & Community Health Services in the Southern Region.

**Joyce J. Fitzpatrick PhD MBA RN FAAN
FNAP** is Elizabeth Brooks Ford Professor of
Nursing, Frances Payne Bolton School of
Nursing, Case Western Reserve University
(CWRU) in Cleveland, Ohio, where she was
Dean from 1982 through 1997. She holds an
adjunct position as Professor, Department
of Geriatrics, Mount Sinai School of
Medicine, New York, NY.

She earned a BSN (Georgetown
University), a MS in Psychiatric-Mental
Health Nursing (Ohio State University), a PhD in Nursing (New
York University), and a MBA (CWRU, 1992). In 1990, Dr.
Fitzpatrick received an honorary doctorate, Doctor of Humane
Letters, from her *alma mater*, Georgetown University, and an
honorary doctorate in 2011 from the Frontier University of
Nursing. She served as a Fulbright Scholar at University College
Cork (UCC), Cork, Ireland during 2007-2008, and has served as a
consultant for publication and research development for UCC.

Professor Fitzpatrick has over 300 publications in nursing and
health care, including 62 books that she has written or edited. She
serves as editor of three major nursing journals: *Applied Nursing
Research, Archives in Psychiatric Nursing* and *Nursing Education
Perspectives,* the official journal of the National League for Nursing.

THE CONTRIBUTORS

Domam Al-Omari BSc MSc

Domam Al-Omari is a staff nurse in a colorectal and hepatobiliary surgical ward at St. Vincent's Private Hospital, Dublin. He has experience in the accident and emergency department, coronary care unit and intensive care unit. He holds a BSc (1996) from the Applied Science University in Jordan, and a MSc (2008) from Trinity College Dublin. At present, Domam is a student in the Doctor of Nursing (DN) programme at University College Cork. His main goal is to complete the DN degree. He plans to apply to a Jordanian university for a teaching post, and to continue researching in the area of pain management.

Saed Azizeh HDIPMH PGDIP (RPN) MSc RGN

Since 2002, Saed has worked as a Senior Nurse in the secure psychiatric acute admission unit in the Dublin North West Mental Health Services. He worked as a Head Nurse in a 24-hour mental handicap centre (1990 to 1996) and in a number of managerial posts in the New Psychiatric Hospital in the United Arab Emirates (1996 to 2002). This included working in the capacity of Senior Charge Nurse in the addiction unit, Nursing Supervisor, and Head Nurse of the forensic unit and the addiction clinic. He became a Registered Psychiatric Nurse after finishing the Postgraduate Diploma in Psychiatric Mental Health Nursing in Dublin City University, Ireland (2009). Saed holds a BSc degree (1990) from the University of Science & Technology, Jordan; a MSc in Public Health (1995); and a Certificate in Forensic Psychiatric Nursing (2004) from the Royal College of Surgeons in Ireland. He is presently a doctoral student (Doctor of Nursing) at the School of Nursing & Midwifery,

University College Cork. Saed's research area relates to investigating the attitudes and knowledge of general nurses working in emergency departments and in general wards towards caring for people presenting with mental health problems. In addition, one of his goals is to apply for a teaching post in a university and to continue to carry out more evidence-based research.

Anne Cleary MSc BA DipMgt RM RGN

Based in the Department of Nursing & Health Care at the Institute of Technology Tralee, Anne has lectured on Nursing, Social Care and Early Childhood Care and Education (ECCE) on the undergraduate BSc Nursing programme since 2003. She trained as a Registered General Nurse in Limerick Regional Hospital and gained her midwifery qualification in St. Munchin's Maternity Hospital, Limerick. She subsequently worked as a qualified nurse/midwife in London and, in Australia, she worked in midwifery, general, medical and orthopaedic nursing. On her return to Ireland, she undertook a BA in Social Care in Waterford Institute of Technology and worked as a residential social care worker in Oberstown Girls Unit for five years. While there, she completed a Postgraduate Diploma in Health Promotion at the University of Limerick and a Master's in Health Promotion in University of Ulster (Jordanstown). She gained valuable experience working as a health promotion officer in Kerry for a further three years. She recently completed a Postgraduate Certificate in University Teaching & Learning at University College Dublin and is a Doctoral student (DN) at the School of Nursing & Midwifery, University College Cork.

Alice Coffey PhD MEd BA Health Management RNT RGN RM

Alice is College Lecturer and Director of Postgraduate Programmes at the Catherine McAuley School of Nursing & Midwifery, University College Cork (UCC). Her clinical experience includes being Clinical Nurse Manager of a rehabilitation unit for older people. Alice is a Lecturer and research supervisor on undergraduate and postgraduate programmes. Her research interests are health and illness transitions for older adults. She was awarded a Clinical Research Fellowship from the Health Research Board. Currently, Alice is involved in research on advance directives with the Department of Gerontology & Rehabilitation. Alice has published in international nursing journals. She is a member of the UCC Ageing Research Cluster and the All Ireland Gerontological Nurses Association.

Nicola Cornally PhD MSc BSc RGN DipNS Cert in Nurse Management

Nicola Cornally is currently a Lecturer at the Catherine McAuley School of Nursing & Midwifery, University College Cork (UCC). Her role includes the co-ordination of e-learning initiatives within the School. For the past number of years, Nicola was employed as a Research Assistant at the School, where she was involved in many projects, including an exploration of the role of the practice nurse and the emergency nurse, from which five articles were published. She is a Registered General Nurse with extensive clinical nursing experience, including general medicine and surgery. Nicola also had the opportunity to work in a senior clinical position in practice development in the acute hospital setting. She holds a MSc in Nursing, a BSc in Nursing Studies, a Diploma in Nursing Science and a Certificate in Nursing Management. Her published MSc thesis explored the attitudes of older adults towards seeking help for chronic pain. For her PhD, Nicola studied help-seeking behaviour for chronic pain, with a particular emphasis on behavioural theory. To date from her thesis, she has published a concept analysis of help-seeking behaviour and an integrative review. Nicola was recently awarded a travel scholarship from the College of Medicine & Health, UCC to attend the European Pain Conference in Germany to present her work. Following the defence of her PhD in 2012, she was made an honorary member of the American Pain Nurses Association for her contribution to pain research. Her research interests include: pain management; chronic pain; theory of planned behaviour; health behaviour; illness behaviour; and professional/practice development.

Mary Rose Day MA BSc HDPHN RPHN RM RGN DipMgt

Mary Rose's nursing experience ranges across diverse areas in acute and community settings as Development Manager Services for Carers, Public Health Nurse, Discharge Co-ordinator and Co-ordinator for Continuing Education & Training, before moving into nurse education as a Lecturer at the Catherine McAuley School of Nursing & Midwifery, University College Cork in 2004. She co-ordinates the Postgraduate Certificate in Community Health Nursing and lectures across postgraduate and undergraduate programmes in nursing. She is currently undertaking a Doctor of Nursing (DN) degree within the School of Nursing. Her research areas include self-neglect in adults and older people, life story work, family carers and community nursing. She has presented papers at international and national conferences in Australia, UK and Ireland and has published in a range of journals.

Mary Ellen Gerardina Harnett-Collins RGN RM RPHN RNT RNP BSc MComm MSc LLB

Gerardina began her career when she trained as a general nurse in the Republic of Ireland (1990). She subsequently worked as an agency nurse in central London. While working in private and public hospitals across the city, she developed a wide experience in population and health care cultures as well as exposure to the social determinants underpinning health. She registered as a midwife in Scotland (1992) and completed a Neonatal Intensive Care Course (1993). She worked in Oxford Maternity Hospital in Liverpool until she began the Higher Diploma in Public Health Nursing at University College Cork (1995). Since then, she has been a practicing public health nurse and is currently part of a team providing 'out of hours' primary, secondary and tertiary nursing care to people in counties Kerry and Cork. In maintaining competence in first aid, she volunteers with the Order of Malta in Killarney and undertakes Pre Hospital Emergency Care Council-accredited certification courses with this organisation. Gerardina has worked as a Lecturer at the Institute of Technology Tralee since 2002 and recently has been appointed

Head of the Department of Nursing. She currently co-ordinates the MSc in Nursing there. Her area of expertise is that of community/public health nursing, primary health care, leadership and policy development. Her aim for the next three years is to develop capability arising out of the Doctor in Nursing degree and to serve as a dedicated professional within the context of practice and learning environments at local, national and international levels.

Catrina Heffernan MSc PGDE BSc RNT RGN

Catrina is a Lecturer in the Institute of Technology Tralee, Co. Kerry. She holds a BSc in Health Studies (West Sussex Institute), a Master's degree in Education (Sheffield Hallam University), a Postgraduate Certificate in Education (Cardiff University) and a Teaching Evidence-based Medicine Certificate (Oxford University). She has held a variety of clinical nursing positions in England. She is a Basic Life Support Instructor with the Irish Heart Foundation and has completed the Advanced Cardiac Life Support Course. Her research areas include those associated with student support, preceptorship and mentorship in education and evidence-based practice. She has published in internationally-recognised nursing journals and is a reviewer for two nursing journals. She was co-founder and a director of a company that provided education, training and consultancy to private and public long-term residential care facilities and day care facilities for the older person and people with special needs. She is presently undertaking a Doctor in Nursing degree at the School of Nursing & Midwifery, University College Cork.

Josephine Hegarty PhD MSc RNT BSc RGN

Josephine is Professor of Nursing within the Catherine McAuley School of Nursing & Midwifery in University College Cork. Her research interests have focused on optimising the experience of the cancer journey for patients and their families. Josephine has been a Cochrane Research Fellow and has completed a Cochrane systematic review on watchful waiting *versus* prostatectomy for prostate cancer. She supervises many PhD and MSc students for their research dissertations. Josephine has published extensively in the international literature.

Sean Kelleher MSc HDip CICN PGDTL BSc RGN

Sean qualified as a Registered General Nurse from the University School of Nursing, Bonn, Germany (1996) and has worked since then in various intensive care units both in Germany and in Ireland. Appointed a Lecturer in the Catherine McAuley School of Nursing & Midwifery, University College Cork (UCC) in 2003, he currently co-ordinates the Post Graduate Diploma in Cardiac & Intensive Care Nursing and leads a number of modules in the undergraduate general nursing programme. Sean's research interests include critical care nursing and issues surrounding student recruitment and international nurse mobility. He has published papers and presented his work at both national and international conferences. Sean is currently leading the development of a new European BSc in Nursing with German programme, in collaboration with the Department of German in UCC, the University Hospital, Bonn, and the German Red Cross (DRK) to educate undergraduate general nursing students in Ireland and Germany. He is also actively involved in establishing EU networks and partners through participation in Leonardo and Erasmus partnership projects. As Chair of the PR committee in the School of Nursing & Midwifery, UCC, Sean is heavily involved in student recruitment activities and projects that enhance the promotion of nursing as a career. He is currently a Doctoral student (DN) at the School of Nursing & Midwifery, UCC.

Patricia Leahy-Warren PhD MSc BSc PG Public Health RPHN RM RGN

Patricia is a Senior Lecturer at the Catherine McAuley School of Nursing & Midwifery in University College Cork. She has a clinical background in general nursing, midwifery and public health nursing and she held posts both nationally and internationally in these areas. She is the recipient of Health Research Board Research Fellowships for both her MSc (Nursing) and her PhD, which was focused on the concept of first-time motherhood. She leads the Maternal & Infant Health Research Team within the School and her research interests are maternal care, postnatal depression, social support, maternal parental self-efficacy, breastfeeding, kangaroo care and public health concerns.

Lynne Marsh MA MSc BSc RNID

Lynne is a College Lecturer in the Catherine McAuley School of Nursing & Midwifery, University College Cork. Her teaching and research is focused on intellectual disability nursing and, through this, she works closely with COPE Foundation in Cork. She is currently undertaking a Doctor of Nursing (DN) degree within the School of Nursing. Her research interests include exploring fathers' experiences of having a child with an intellectual disability, health needs of people with intellectual disabilities and reusable learning outcomes (RLOs).

Omar Melhem MSc BSc

Omar has worked as a staff nurse in Jordan, Australia and Ireland. Currently, he works as a Senior Nurse in Connolly Hospital, Blanchardstown, Dublin. He started his nursing career in 1999, when he was working at the University Hospital, Amman, Jordan as a Staff Nurse in the accident and emergency department. In 2000, he moved to Dublin and started work at Connolly Hospital. Between 2005 and 2006, he moved to Sydney, Australia and worked at the Prince of Wales Hospital as a Charge Nurse before moving back to Dublin. He obtained his Bachelor of Nursing Science (BSc) degree from the University of Science & Technology, Jordan (1999) and a MSc in (2004). His areas of expertise are respiratory nursing (COPD care) and diabetes care. His current professional goal is to complete his Doctor of Nursing degree (DN) and work as a lecturer. Because he is interested in COPD patients' care, his proposed research will focus on symptom burden and quality of life for patients with end-stage COPD.

Malitha Veera Monis RGN RM BSc MSc

Malitha was born in India and has spent the past few years working in Ireland. After completing her BSc in Nursing degree in the College of Nursing, Bangalore, India, she spent time working as a Clinical Instructor (1996 to 1999) and as Principal of Alva's School of Nursing (1999 to 2002), which involved various educational, managerial, and administrative roles. In 2004, she completed a MSc in Midwifery at Manipal College of Nursing, India. Subsequently, Malitha worked as a Lecturer in Laxmi Memorial College of Nursing, teaching graduate and postgraduate students. In 2007, Malitha came to Cork, in order to gain international clinical experience and currently she works as a Staff Midwife in Cork University Maternity Hospital. Her goal is to become a Clinical Midwife Practitioner, and to engage herself further in research. She is presently a Doctoral student (Doctor of Nursing) at the School of Nursing & Midwifery, University College Cork. Her main research interest is concerned with the effects of medical termination of pregnancy.

Margaret M. Murphy MSc BSc PGDip Teaching & Learning RM RGN Cert. in Intensive Care Nursing Cert. in Nursing Management International Board Certified Lactation Consultant

Margaret is a Lecturer/Practitioner in the Catherine McAuley School of Nursing & Midwifery, University College Cork since 2007. She graduated as a Registered General Nurse in 1989 and worked as a nurse in adult intensive care over the next 10 years. She graduated as a Registered Midwife (1996) and, from 1999 to 2007, worked within the Cork maternity services as a Midwife, Clinical Midwife Manager and Midwife Tutor. She is involved with multidisciplinary colleagues in delivering the NRP and PROMPT programmes at Cork University Maternity Hospital (CUMH). As a Lecturer/Practitioner, she carries a clinical caseload supporting students while they are on placement and providing antenatal breastfeeding classes to women in CUMH. She has an active publication profile and is a Doctor of Nursing (DN) student at University College Cork. Her research focus is the investigation of subsequent pregnancy after pregnancy loss. She has presented her research at national and international conferences, including ICM (2008). She is a member of the Maternal and Infant Research strand in the School of Nursing & Midwifery. She is a member of the International Lactation Consultants Association, the Association of Lactation Consultants of Ireland and the National Midwifery Lecturers Network. She is a peer reviewer for the *Journal of Human Lactation* and *The Practising Midwife*. She is a staunch advocate for women and believes that, together, women and midwives can improve pregnancy and birth outcomes to create a healthier society for all.

Sinéad O'Sullivan MSc BSc RGN

Sinéad trained as a Registered General Nurse in St. John's Hospital, Limerick, where she gained experience in medical, surgical and gynaecological nursing. She has worked as a Clinical Nurse Manager II in Care of the Older Adult in Milford Care Centre, Limerick since 2003. She undertook a Bachelor of Science in Nursing in University of Limerick (2001); a Graduate Diploma (Rehabilitation of the Older Person) at the University of Limerick (2010); a MSc in Nursing (Rehabilitation of the Older Person) (2011); and is currently undertaking a Doctor of Nursing in University College Cork. Sinéad served on the Executive Council of the Federation of Catholic Voluntary Nursing Homes from 2006 to 2009, serving as Vice-Chairperson for one year. Her goal is to increase her research capacity in care of the older adult in residential care and her vision is to make a difference in the discipline by assuming a leadership role within the clinical area of care of the older adult.

Eileen Savage PhD MEd BDN RGN RSCN

Eileen is a Professor of Nursing at the Catherine McAuley School of Nursing & Midwifery, University College Cork. She is actively involved in research and teaching. Her teaching interests are in research methodology, evidence-based practice and children's nursing and health care. She leads a research programme on chronic illness management, with a special interest in the areas of self- and family management. She has conducted a number of funded research projects, and works with national and international collaborators. Her work has been published in the international peer-reviewed literature.

Elizabeth Weathers BSc RGN

Elizabeth Weathers is a Registered General Nurse with clinical experience within both the acute and community care settings. She has a particular interest in spiritual care, palliative care, chronic illness, and gerontology. Elizabeth has been employed as a part-time Research Assistant within the School of Nursing & Midwifery, University College Cork (UCC) since April 2011. In her role as Research Assistant, she has been involved in many projects, including international studies investigating nurses' preferred end-of-life treatment options, nursing knowledge of advance directives, and nursing descriptions of caring. In 2010, Elizabeth was awarded a Dr. H.H. Steward Nursing Scholarship by the National University of Ireland for her academic achievements. In 2011, she registered for a Master's (Research) degree but in October 2012 converted to a PhD following the guidance of her supervisors. Her research is focused on the concept of spirituality and is due for completion in 2014. She has published in international journals and presented her work at international conferences. Elizabeth was recently awarded a travel scholarship from the College of Medicine & Health, UCC and will present her work at the International Conference on Ageing & Spirituality in Edinburgh in July. She is a trained facilitator of the Hospice Friendly Hospitals Final Journeys Programme and has facilitated the programme for undergraduate nursing students within the School.

Teresa Wills MSc BSc RGN

Teresa is a College Lecturer in the Catherine McAuley School of Nursing & Midwifery, University College Cork (UCC). She is involved in the delivery and development of both undergraduate and postgraduate nurse education. Teresa coordinates the Postgraduate Diploma/ Certificate Programmes in  Gerontological Nursing. Prior to this, she was a Clinical Placement Co-ordinator and Nurse Tutor in the Bon Secours Hospital, Cork. She is a member of the Health Ageing Research Theme and the ISS21 Ageing Cluster group within the University. She is currently undertaking a Doctor of Nursing (DN) degree within the School of Nursing & Midwifery, UCC. Her research interests include the older adult, obesity, complementary therapies and hand-washing. She has published and presented papers at national and international conferences.

LEADERSHIP IN ACTION

Influential Irish Women Nurses' Contribution to Society

Geraldine McCarthy and Joyce J. Fitzpatrick
(Editors)

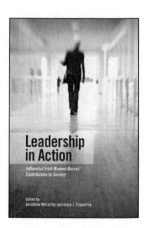

This book is both a testimony to the 20 Irish women who made a difference in society through their significant leadership contributions, and a book that can be used to teach aspiring leaders.

LEADERSHIP IN ACTION profiles 20 Irish women leaders who began their careers as nurses and went forward to make outstanding contributions in many aspects of Irish society, outside of and within the profession.

Their stories of success will help not only students in nursing, but also future leaders in other disciplines, to chart new courses in their life's work and to build on the holistic, caring, interpersonal skills that are at the core of their nursing preparation.

Each of the profiles includes the early influences and major life events that shaped the leader; the person's vision for their life work; their competencies, strengths and values; the significant challenges that they experienced; opportunities that enhanced their success; their perspective on the characteristics of leaders; and their advice to aspiring leaders. Importantly, these profiles provide a snapshot in time of the significant contributions of these leaders.

Available from Oak Tree Press (www.oaktreepress.com) in print and ebook editions.